Decades of American History

AMERICA IN THE 1920s

MICHAEL J. O'NEAL

Facts On File, Inc.

For Emma and Grace, with the hope that your bright futures include time for a backward glance at your country's rich and exciting history.

A Stonesong Press Book
Decades of American History: *America in the 1920s*

Facts On File, Inc.
132 West 31st Street
New York NY 10001

Library of Congress Cataloging-in-Publication Data

O'Neal, Michael J., 1949–
  America in the 1920s / Michael J. O'Neal.
       p. cm. — (Decades of American history)
  "A Stonesong Press book."
  Includes bibliographical references (p.   ) and index.
  Audience: Grades 4–9.
  ISBN 0-8160-5637-4 (acid-free paper)
1. United States—History—1919-1933—Juvenile literature. 2. Nineteen twenties—Juvenile literature.   I. Title. II. Series.
  E784.O54 2005
  973.91'5—dc22   2004018947

Facts On File books are available at special discounts when purchased in bulk quantities for businesses, associations, institutions, or sales promotions. Please call our Special Sales Department in New York at (212) 967-8800 or (800) 322-8755.

You can find Facts On File on the World Wide Web at http://www.factsonfile.com

Text design by Laura Smyth, Smythetype
Photo research by Larry Schwartz
Cover design by Pehrsson Design

Printed in the United States of America

VB PKG 10 9 8 7 6 5 4 3 2 1

This book is printed on acid-free paper.

CONTENTS

CHAPTER 1

USHERING IN A NEW DECADE, 1920

LIFE IN THE UNITED STATES FROM 1920 to 1930 seems as though it must have been lively and carefree. The nation was at peace. The standard of living was rising through much of the period, and Americans seemed to have more than enough money. For many people, it was a time of fun and a new feeling of personal freedom. When they were not dancing to popular music, they were taking to the road in their new cars or finding other ways to enjoy themselves. The decade's very nickname—the Roaring Twenties—is still used to suggest the seemingly free and easy life that Americans lived then.

Many Americans protested the passage of the Eighteenth Amendment, banning the manufacture, sale, and transportation of liquor.
(Library of Congress)

Chicago's Al Capone was one of the most notorious gangsters and bootleggers of the 1920s. *(Library of Congress)*

The word *bootleg* as a term for illegal liquor originated in the 19th century, with pioneers who broke the law by selling whiskey to American Indians. They developed a type of flat bottle that could be easily hidden in the leg of a boot; thus, they were bootleggers.

Mention the 1920s, and Americans form a variety of pictures: To some, it was the era of big-city gangsters, such as Al Capone. Capone and other mobsters defied Prohibition and made fortunes selling illegal bootleg liquor. They were called bootleggers because they and their customers often hid flasks of liquor in their high boots. They were criminals, but their daring defiance of the law turned them into almost romantic figures to many.

To others, it was an era of such industrial giants as Henry Ford. Ford's popular Model T automobile helped end the isolation of rural life, gave people more personal freedom, and transformed Americans into a people constantly on the move.

Still others picture the flapper. This was the name given to a new type of woman who defied the conventions of her mother and grandmother. To her elders, the flapper was shocking because of her poise, boldness, and freedom in dress and manners.

For some Americans, music defines the 1920s. The decade witnessed the boom of jazz and of uninhibited dance crazes such as the Charleston. Another dance craze, the Lindy Hop, reflected the reputation of aviation hero Charles ("Lindy") Lindbergh, who made the first solo airplane flight across the Atlantic Ocean.

Finally, the Roaring Twenties was the decade when Americans' demand for entertainment exploded. The silent films of earlier years gave way to the talkies, or movies with synchronized sound. Americans followed the careers and love lives of wildly adored film stars, including Clara Bow, Douglas Fairbanks, and John Barrymore. Equally adored were colorful sports figures whose names remain legendary, including Babe Ruth in baseball, Jack Dempsey in boxing, Bobby Jones in golf, and the Four Horsemen of Notre Dame in football.

The events of history do not always correspond neatly with the dates on a calendar. The 1920s are no exception. The political events and social trends that defined the 1920s began somewhat earlier, with the end

WILSON'S BIGGEST OPPONENT

Republican Henry Cabot Lodge (1850–1924) served as a senator from 1893 until his death. He was a consistent opponent of Wilson's liberal ideas, and he led the fight against the League of Nations. In a speech on August 12, 1919, he expressed his opposition to the League of Nations in these words: "I have never had but one allegiance—I cannot divide it now. I have loved but one flag and I cannot share that devotion and give affection to the mongrel banner invented for a league. Internationalism, illustrated by the Bolshevik and by the men to whom all countries are alike provided they can make money out of them, is to me repulsive." (The word *Bolshevik* comes from the Russian word for "greater." The Bolsheviks, or Bolshevists, were the radical wing of the Russian Social Democratic party. To many people, the word was and still is synonymous with *communist,* referring to a system in which the state owns all private property. The very word evoked fear for many Americans in the 1920s.)

Other dance crazes of the 1920s included the Black Bottom, the Shimmy, the Texas Tommy, the Turkey Trot, the Bunny Hug, and the Two-Fist Stomp.

of World War I in late 1918. In the wake of that war, President Woodrow Wilson (1856–1924) failed to persuade the U.S. Congress to vote in favor of joining the League of Nations as a way to prevent future wars. Ten years later, the Roaring Twenties came to a spectacular end. In October 1929, the stock market crashed, the economy began to collapse, and the Great Depression of the 1930s began.

The decade of the 1920s thus started with dashed hopes for future world peace and ended with dark fears of economic ruin. Sandwiched between these events was a period of rapid economic growth, increasing affluence (for some Americans, at least), and momentous changes in American society. These changes made the 1920s the first modern decade. It was the decade that marked the start of a shift from the rural, small-town values of the 19th and early 20th centuries to those of the more urban, industrial, and technological world of today. To some observers, though, it was also a decade of greed, excess, and materialism.

The population of the United States in 1920 was about 105.7 million. By 1930 the number had risen to about 123.2 million.

Anti-German sentiment was shown in a number of ways. In St. Paul, Minnesota, the Germania Life Insurance Building was renamed the Guardian Building, and its statue of Germania, clad as a female warrior, was taken down. The term *hot dog* was adopted to replace *frankfurter,* a word derived from the German city Frankfurt. Similarly, *Salisbury steak,* a British name, was used instead of *hamburger,* derived from the German city Hamburg.

THE LAST YEARS OF THE WILSON PRESIDENCY

World War I

To understand the mind-set of Americans in the Roaring Twenties, it is necessary to understand their attitudes both during World War I (1914–18) and in the immediate aftermath of the war. For in many ways, Americans' outlook in the 1920s was a reaction against these earlier years.

Woodrow Wilson had taken office in 1913. The following year, World War I began in Europe. This war pitted the Central Powers, chiefly Germany and the Austro-Hungarian Empire, against the Allied Powers, including Great Britain, France, and Russia. During the early years of the war, Wilson tried to keep the United States out of the war, which seemed to be yet another in an endless procession of European conflicts dating back centuries.

But events forced Wilson's hand. Germany refused to recognize U.S. neutrality. Its submarines sank American ships in the Atlantic, and hundreds of American lives were lost. In light of these and other events, pressure for U.S. entry into the war mounted. Finally Wilson felt that the United States had no choice but to come to the aid of its European allies. In April 1917, the United States declared war on Germany.

The nation quickly mobilized for war, and the Wilson administration was masterful at convincing the majority of Americans that war was the only option. Some Americans steadfastly opposed U.S. involvement in the war. They believed that it was being fought only to protect U.S. economic interests and not for higher principles. Most Americans, though, supported the president in his belief that the war had to be fought, as he put it, to "make the world safe for democracy." Most willingly accepted the sacrifices that had to be made. They responded enthusiastically to

African-American soldiers dig a trench in a French cemetery for the burial of American soldiers killed during World War I. *(Library of Congress)*

Wilson's call for Wheatless Mondays and Meatless Tuesdays to conserve food supplies, especially for the troops. Boy Scouts planted backyard vegetable gardens. Chicago homemakers were so successful at using leftovers that the volume of trash in that city dropped by a third within a year. Americans became, like their president, idealistic.

Some of the sacrifices, though, entailed the loss of civil liberties, especially freedom of speech. The 1917 Espionage Act imposed stiff fines and jail terms on anyone found guilty of aiding the enemy or obstructing the recruitment of soldiers. The 1918 Sedition Act made it a crime to discourage the sale of bonds used to finance the war or to make statements critical of the government. More than 2,000 people were eventually prosecuted under these laws, and many of those were

"I glanced at my watch. One minute to 11:00, thirty seconds, fifteen. And then it was 11:00 A.M., the eleventh hour of the eleventh day of the eleventh month.... Star shells, rockets and flares began to go up, and I turned my ship toward the field. The war was over."

—Eddie Rickenbacker, American air ace, describing the moment of armistice from 500 feet above no-man's land at Conflans, France, on November 11, 1918

Many people at the time believed that it was unconstitutional for a sitting president to leave American soil. President Wilson was the first president in history to do so.

deported (that is, sent back to their native countries). Movies were censored for so-called un-American content. In this climate, hostility toward foreigners, particularly Germans, was rampant.

When the United States entered the war in Europe, the fighting had been at a brutal stalemate for more than two years. When hostilities finally ended on November 11, 1918, the United States had lost more than 112,000 soldiers. These losses, though, were almost trivial compared to the losses suffered by the European nations. Young men by the thousands had been slaughtered as they hurled themselves against enemy positions they could not hope to capture. The British lost nearly a million, the French 1.38 million, and Germany 1.8 million. Starvation and homelessness were commonplace, and social order in many places was nonexistent. Wilson, considered among the most intellectual and idealistic presidents in American history, fervently sought a way to ensure that the Great War would be the "war to end all wars," in his words.

The Aftermath of War

Wilson traveled to France himself to negotiate the Treaty of Versailles, which officially ended the war and redrew the map of Europe. He came to the negotiations with high ideals. Despite these ideals, though, the treaty that he helped negotiate was ultimately a failure, largely because it blamed Germany and its allies entirely for the war. It required Germany to pay the Allies $56 billion in reparations, or compensation for how much the war cost. Germany was able to pay only part of the money, but the reparations clause of the treaty ruined the nation's economy and left Germans feeling humiliated.

The treaty Wilson negotiated consisted of what he called the Fourteen Points. The most important of the Fourteen Points was the last. This was a provision that called for the formation of the League of Nations, an international body similar to today's United Nations.

Wilson believed that the League of Nations would settle many of the disputes that remained unresolved both by the war and by the rest of the treaty. Most important, he believed that it would help prevent future wars.

After returning home, Wilson had to win the support of Congress for the treaty and the League of Nations. What followed was an intense and exhausting political struggle. Many Americans and their representatives were tired of entanglements with other nations. They did not believe that the hands of the United States should be tied by an international organization. They were even growing tired of Wilson's idealism and felt that the president was constantly preaching to them. Many Americans found the bookish Wilson stiff-necked and overly pious.

While Wilson could count on the support of fellow Democrats in Congress, he failed to win over enough Republicans to get the necessary two-thirds majority vote to approve the treaty. The United States never became a member of the League of Nations. Only a 1921 joint resolution by the Senate and the House of Representatives officially ended the war with the Central Powers. Wilson had failed in the endeavor that perhaps meant more to him than anything else he did in office.

In the midst of the struggle for ratification, or congressional approval, of the treaty, Wilson traveled to the American West to try to win support for the league from the American people. While he was in Pueblo, Colorado, he became very ill. He was rushed back to Washington, D.C., and had a serious stroke on October 2, 1919. For the remainder of his term he was in poor health. Today it seems unimaginable, but in an era before 24-hour news networks, the administration was able to hide the 28th president's condition from the American public. For the next 17 months, Wilson's wife, Edith Bolling Galt Wilson, was what has been called the 28th-and-a-half president. She reviewed all the correspondence and official papers that came into the White House. She emerged from the

Versailles, located near Paris, is a magnificent palace built by King Louis XIV. Construction began in 1664 and continued until just before his death in 1715. The Treaty of Versailles was signed in the palace's famous Hall of Mirrors.

President Woodrow Wilson rides with his wife, Edith Bolling Galt Wilson, to the president's second inauguration in 1917.
(Library of Congress)

The treaty ending World War I was signed at the magnificent palace of Versailles, near Paris, France. *(Library of Congress)*

"I am for any kind of insurance against a barbaric reversal of civilization."

—Woodrow Wilson, speech delivered during the summer 1919 western campaign in support of the League of Nations

Leading the fight for a prohibition amendment was the Women's Christian Temperance Union (WCTU), formed in 1873. When the Eighteenth Amendment was passed, the WCTU was under the leadership of Anna Gordon (1853–1931), who then urged the WCTU to turn to other social problems.

president's sickroom with notes that claimed to express the president's wishes on matters of state. She even made cabinet appointments. Wilson's collapse seemed almost symbolic of the fatigue that had overtaken Americans as the new decade began.

Disillusionment

Though the war had ended, the world was shaken by the destruction and loss of life that had resulted. Adding to Americans' misery was the flu epidemic of 1918, which claimed 20 million lives worldwide and a half million lives in the United States—a thousand in one day in Philadelphia, Pennsylvania.

In many ways, life in the 1920s United States was a reaction against these wearying events. Americans tried to escape the shadow of the war by almost denying that it had taken place. People who had shared Wilson's idealism and willingness to sacrifice during the war became more cynical and materialistic. A generation of young writers and thinkers who had fought in the war survived only to tell of its horror and brutality. The progressive ideals Wilson and others held during the 1910s seemed dead; the community spirit of the war gave way to what President Herbert Hoover at the end of the decade would call "rugged individualism." Americans were sick of the turmoil, uncertainty, and fear of the war years and their immediate aftermath. They were ready to have fun, and by the end of the decade nearly everyone had caught the spirit of the times by singing the words to Eddie Cantor's famous 1928 song, "Makin' Whoopee."

THE EIGHTEENTH AND NINETEENTH AMENDMENTS

During the last years of the Wilson presidency, two amendments to the U.S. Constitution were passed. Both would have a major effect on the social and cultural life of the nation during the 1920s. The first, creating Prohibition, was the result of a small-town religious outlook. It has been called the victory of the village over the big city. The other, granting women the right to vote, was the outcome of a more modern, nonreligious point of view. The two amendments embody the contradictions of life in the Roaring Twenties.

Prohibition

The temperance movement against alcohol consumption began in the 19th century, when reformers attacked the demand for liquor by urging people to give up drinking. But after the start of the 20th century, the reformers began to put more effort into stopping the supply of liquor. They backed state laws restricting the sale of alcohol and shutting down saloons. By 1914, 14 states had adopted some form of prohibition; they were called dry states. By 1919 that number had risen to 26. During World War I, the Anti-Saloon League was able to get various federal laws against alcohol passed. These laws were intended to preserve the morals of young American servicemen and to conserve grain for food. (With some exceptions, most liquor is made

Women frequently led the fight against liquor, as shown in this temperance poster.
(Library of Congress)

Eddie Cantor (1892–1964) was born Isadore Itzkowitz, and in his early teens he supported himself as a singer at New York's Coney Island, where his piano player was Jimmy Durante. Durante went on to become a famous performer and comedian on the vaudeville stage, on radio, and in the early days of television.

Eddie Cantor was a popular singer known especially for his 1928 song "Makin' Woopee."
(Private Collection)

ROARING SLANG

The 1920s was perhaps the first youth-oriented period in American history, and the decade produced a great deal of slang. Expressions dating to the 1920s or that became popular during the decade and that are still sometimes used today include *Joe College, blind date, screwy, wet blanket, ritzy, jeepers creepers, jalopy, dough* (money), *baloney* (nonsense), *For crying out loud!,* and *None of your beeswax!*

Here are some common 1920s slang expressions that are no longer widely used but still colorful:

Bee's knees or *cat's meow:* terrific, great
Get a wiggle on!: "Get a move on!"; "Let's get going!"
Glad rags: fancy clothes for going out on the town
Hip to the jive: cool, trendy
Iron one's shoelaces: go to the restroom.

from grain crops.) By this time, the members of Congress from dry states outnumbered those from wet states two to one.

The result was the Eighteenth Amendment to the Constitution. This amendment was ratified by the necessary two-thirds majority of the states in late 1919. It placed a national ban on the "manufacture, sale, or transportation of intoxicating liquors," though it did not make it illegal to buy or drink liquor. To enforce the amendment, Congress passed the National Prohibition Enforcement Act, commonly called the Volstead Act, on October 28, 1919. President Wilson vetoed the bill, but Congress overrode the veto (that is, voted to enact the law despite the president's veto).

Many people praised the Prohibition amendment. They noted that arrests for drunkenness declined sharply, reducing the costs of maintaining jails and prisons. Medical statistics showed a steep drop in the number of people treated for alcohol-related diseases. But even during the 1920s, the experiment was regarded as a failure. For one thing, the laws were nearly impossible to enforce. A great deal of illegal alcohol entered the country from Canada and Mexico. The number of U.S. Treasury Department agents assigned to enforce the law was woefully small. Their low pay made them easy targets for bribery by bootleggers who continued to make and sell liquor. While many rural areas of the country remained dry, drinking continued in most of the big cities. Colorful newspaper stories about federal raids on speakeasies, or hidden clubs where drinking took place, were common. (The clubs were called speakeasies because patrons were urged to talk in a low volume, or speak easy, so the police would not hear them and raid the club.) But these

A common slang term for bootleg liquor was *coffin varnish* because much of the liquor contained poisonous ingredients, such as lye or lead, that lingered in the makeshift containers used in distilling. The worst danger was wood, or methyl, alcohol, a poison that causes blindness and death.

Italian immigrant Angelo Siciliano, who gained fame as Charles Atlas, promised American men that he could help them gain perfect muscular physiques.
(Private Collection)

The nation's first Miss America, sixteen-year-old Margaret Gorman, won the crown in 1921. *(Library of Congress)*

"The Eighteenth Amendment... is the most benevolent... the most far-reaching reform ever inaugurated by any people anywhere in the history of the world and any man who sneers at it is an enemy of God."

—Reverend Arthur James Barton, D.D., chairman of the executive committee of the Anti-Saloon League of America

MISS AMERICA AND CHARLES ATLAS

The Miss America pageant began in Atlantic City, New Jersey, in 1921. A new emphasis on beauty and physical appearance, though, was not limited to women. A year later Charles Atlas won the title of the World's Most Perfectly Developed Man. Atlas built his reputation in part on his claim—false, as it turned out—that he had been a "97-pound weakling."

stories only enhanced the appeal of these places to urban customers who saw themselves as sophisticated members of the smart set. Even today, the speakeasy remains a symbol of the excess of the Roaring Twenties, though the percentage of Americans who went to them was probably quite small.

The ink was barely dry on the Eighteenth Amendment and the Volstead Act when calls for repeal (or cancellation) of the amendment began. The 1920s was an era of growing personal freedom. The development and spread of the radio, the automobile, the telephone, and motion pictures heightened this sense of freedom. Many Americans quickly came to believe that the federal government had no business regulating personal habits. They became cynical about a law that the government seemed to have no power to enforce and were thus cynical about government in general.

Beginning in 1922, the Association against the Prohibition Amendment supported candidates for office who favored the repeal of Prohibition. They found allies in the Women's Organization for National Prohibition Reform—in marked contrast to the many women's groups that had fought for temperance and prohibition in earlier years. The movement gained momentum throughout the decade, and in 1933, the Twenty-first Amendment to the Constitution was ratified, repealing the Eighteenth. Liquor laws were once again in the hands of the states rather than the federal government.

Women's Suffrage

If the Eighteenth Amendment was an attempt to restrict and control personal behavior, the Nineteenth Amendment, granting women the right to vote in all elections, was a major step in freeing half the American population.

Campaigns for women's suffrage, or the right to vote, had dated back to at least the mid-19th century. Throughout the rest of the 19th century and during the early 20th century, thousands of women conducted hundreds of campaigns to gain the right to vote. Under the influence of Progressive politicians such as Woodrow Wilson, the movement gained momentum during the 1910s. During World War I, women had served ably in Europe as nurses. Many women on the home front gained respect by working in jobs that had formerly been held by servicemen who were off fighting in the war. Finally, the time had come for women.

Early in 1919, the House of Representatives passed the Nineteenth Amendment by a vote of 304 to 90; the Senate approved the amendment by a vote of 56 to 25.

After decades of campaigns, marches, and rallies, women "suffragettes," or suffragists, finally gained for women the right to vote with the passage of the Nineteenth Amendment. *(Library of Congress)*

Other states were much slower to ratify the Nineteenth Amendment; Maryland, for instance, did not ratify it until 1941 and, oddly, did not send official notification that it had done so to Washington, D.C., until 1958.

Nellie Taylor Ross of Wyoming was the nation's first woman governor. *(AP/Wide World Photos)*

In Tennessee, the Nineteenth Amendment passed by just a single vote when a 24-year-old legislator, Harry Burn, voted in favor of the amendment after his mother scolded him for initially opposing it.

WOMEN IN GOVERNMENT

In 1925, the nation's first woman governor was elected, Nellie Taylor Ross of Wyoming. For all its rough-and-tumble, Wild West image, Wyoming was perhaps the most progressive state when it came to women's suffrage. Wyoming granted women the right to vote in state and local elections in 1869 when it was still a territory. It refused to join the Union unless it could keep this provision in its laws. Many historians believe that Wyoming allowed women the right to vote as a way to attract women to the state during a time when the state's population of miners, ranchers, and cowboys was overwhelmingly male.

Thirty-six states needed to ratify the amendment for it to become part of the Constitution. Illinois, Wisconsin, and Michigan were the first ones. The 36th was Tennessee, whose state legislature voted to ratify the amendment on August 18, 1920. The Nineteenth Amendment, which said that "The right of citizens of the United States to vote shall not be denied or abridged by the United States or by any State on account of sex," became part of the U.S. Constitution.

In 1920, Americans were tired of war, turmoil, and the political seriousness of Wilson's two terms in office. The nation was ready for a return to normality. That is what the nation's new president promised.

CHAPTER 2

THE ELECTION OF WARREN HARDING, 1920–1921

Incoming president Warren G. Harding (right) rides to his inauguration with outgoing president Woodrow Wilson on March 4, 1921. *(Library of Congress)*

MARCH 4, 1921, WAS INAUGURATION Day in Washington, D.C. Under a sunny sky, two men rode in the back of a Pierce-Arrow cabriolet—an open touring car—to Capitol Hill. One was the outgoing president, Woodrow Wilson. The other was a man whom Wilson despised, the newly elected 29th president, Warren Gamaliel Harding.

The presence of the two men side by side, one giving place to the other, seemed symbolic of the changes that would take place in U.S. society during the Roaring Twenties. The Great War under Wilson had forced Americans to be dutiful, idealistic, patriotic,

Warren Harding married Florence Mabel Kling, whose sharp, domineering personality earned her the nickname "the Duchess." *(Library of Congress)*

For the first time in the event's history, loudspeakers were used at Harding's inauguration.

and self-sacrificing. Harding led the way into a new decade in which many Americans became materialistic, isolationist (not wanting to become involved in foreign affairs), cynical, and concerned with the here and now rather than high ideals.

HARDING'S BACKGROUND

The new president could not have been more unlike the old. Wilson, who had suffered a stroke in 1919, was frail and shrunken. His hands gripped a cane, and he was almost an invalid. He looked pale and tense as he rode to the inauguration. Harding, in contrast, was robust—some would say even handsome. The public seemed to have elected Harding not because he had any particular qualifications for the presidency but simply because they liked him. They had grown weary of Wilson, who was always interested in a cause.

While Wilson was scholarly and intellectual—he had been president of Princeton University—Harding was easygoing and kindly. During his presidency, anyone could walk into the White House and shake his hand, and he often stayed up late at night answering mail from ordinary citizens. While Wilson was straightlaced, Harding loved nothing as much as a good poker game or drinking with his friends. On the day after the election, when he learned that he had won, rather than getting down to work he had played a round of golf. Wilson had been the nation's schoolmaster, rapping its knuckles with his ruler. Harding was more like a playground pal who sometimes made mischief but was never a bully. Ordinary Americans thought that Harding was like them and that they could trust him in matters of state.

Little in Harding's background suggested that he was destined for the highest office in the land. He was born near Blooming Grove, Ohio, in 1865. After graduating from nearby Ohio Central College at age 17, he tried selling hardware, then insurance. But his real love, he knew, was the newspaper business. He had edited a student newspaper in college, and after the family had moved to Marion, Ohio, he found a job with a local newspaper. In 1884, he and two friends put up $300 to buy the *Marion Daily Star,* which was about to collapse. The town's population was only 4,500, and Harding faced competition from two other papers, but he managed to make a go of it. By 1890, he had bought out his two partners. Actually, he had won one partner's share of the business on the strength of a good poker hand.

In 1891, Harding married Florence Mabel Kling, daughter of Marion's richest citizen. If people liked Warren, the same could not be said of Florence, who was five years older than her husband and a divorcée. Her father cut her off because he believed that Harding had black ancestors, and when he referred to Harding, he often used a racial slur. He even tried to run Harding out of business. In opposing her father, Florence had developed a sharp, domineering personality. Harding—and soon the American public—called her the Duchess. She became the financial brains behind the *Daily Star* and in the 1890s turned it into a profitable success. In time, she also pushed Harding into politics.

Harding enjoyed hanging around with the local members of the Republican Party, and they liked him because of his easygoing manner. So with their support, he was elected to two terms in the Ohio State Senate (1900–1904). He also served one term (1904–1906) as lieutenant governor. In 1910, he ran for governor of Ohio but lost. Then in 1914 he was elected to the U.S. Senate. His record as a senator was entirely undistinguished. He voted with his party 95 percent of the time—when he voted, that is, for he was absent

Warren Harding was the first-ever sitting U.S. senator to be elected to the presidency. He was the first president to ride to his inauguration in a car. And he was the first president to have been born after the end of the Civil War.

"I never wore a wedding ring. I don't like badges. And perhaps it's just a crotchet of a woman who knows women's province but insists on having a personality…I do not like to cook. I hate fussing with food…I love business."

—First Lady Florence Harding

Florence Harding was a great believer in astrology. Her astrologer, known as Madame Marcia, had predicted that Warren would win high office but that he would meet a "sudden, violent, or peculiar death." She turned out to be right.

"BLOVIATION"

Even Harding recognized that his oratory was sometimes overblown. He often used the slang term *bloviate,* meaning to talk in high-flown phrases, to describe his style. Journalists and writers loved to make fun of his phrasing. H. L. Mencken, a prominent journalist, wrote that Harding's English "reminds me of a string of wet sponges." When Harding died, poet e.e. cummings wrote: "The only man, woman, or child who ever wrote a simple declarative sentence with seven grammatical errors is dead."

when the roll was called 40 percent of the time. He avoided voting on touchy subjects, including the bill to grant women the right to vote. His name appears as a sponsor on 134 bills, but 122 of them dealt purely with local Ohio issues; the 12 national bills that bore his name were for such things as celebrating the anniversary of the Pilgrims' landing.

THE RETURN TO "NORMALCY"

Nonetheless, in 1919, Harding's Ohio political crony Harry M. Daugherty began a campaign to get Harding elected president. At the Republican National Convention in Chicago, Illinois, in the summer of 1920, at least three other candidates stood a better chance of winning the party's nomination for president. The problem was that the convention remained deadlocked. In ballot after ballot, none of the three emerged as the winner. So the party bosses met at Chicago's Blackstone Hotel and worked out a deal. The next day, after the 10th ballot, Harding was the party's nominee.

That year the Democrats nominated James M. Cox. Cox, whose vice presidential candidate was future president Franklin D. Roosevelt, was a colorless candidate who stood no chance against the likable Harding. Harding won the election with a convincing 61 percent of the vote. While his margin of victory was the largest in a century, voter turnout, just 49.3 percent, was the smallest in American history to that time.

Harding won in spite of a campaign speaking style that was somewhat pompous. He often made blunders. On one occasion he made reference to Shakespeare's play *Charles the V;* unfortunately for Harding, Shakespeare never wrote such a play. He was also fond of speaking in overblown alliterative phrases (phrases that repeat initial letters). In one campaign speech, on May 14, 1920, in Boston, he made his most famous statement, one that reflected his attitude about the role of government in the postwar years and that perfectly shows his style.

Intellectuals scorned Harding's style. William Gibbs McAdoo, a Democratic Party leader, said that a Harding speech was like "an army of pompous phrases moving across the landscape in search of an idea." Many pointed out that there was no such word as *normalcy* and that he should have said "normality." But Harding had shrewdly caught the spirit of the American people. They were ready for normalcy.

A NEW ROLE FOR WOMEN

The 1920 presidential election was the first in which women could vote. Women's organizations, though, were disappointed that only about 26 percent of eligible women voted. Like men that year, they tended to vote along party lines and voted for Harding in about the same proportion as male voters did.

The passage of the Nineteenth Amendment was a first step in the liberation of women during the 1920s. After the sacrifices of the war years, young people, especially young women, wanted to break free from the restrictions of the Victorian age, named for English

"America's present need is not heroics, but healing… not surgery, but serenity; not the dramatic, but the dispassionate; not experiment, but equipoise; not submergence in internationality, but sustainment in triumphant nationality."

—Warren Harding

First Lady Florence Harding operates a movie camera at the White House. *(Library of Congress)*

FLORENCE THE FIRST

Florence Harding was the first first lady ever to fly in an airplane and the first to hold her own press conference, though all the reporters were women. She spoke out in favor of equality of opportunity for women in sports, employment, and politics. She was the driving force behind the founding of the first penitentiary for women that was designed to rehabilitate rather than just punish.

"The creation and fulfillment of a successful home is a bit of craftsmanship that compares favorably with building a beautiful cathedral."

—An editor in
The Ladies Home Journal, 1922

Queen Victoria's long 19th-century reign. Unlike her mother, who dressed in dark, restrictive, modest clothing and strove to conduct herself with complete respectability, the flapper of the 1920s was determined to express herself. While not all women became flappers, most were influenced by the trends set by the flapper outlook prevalent in big cities and on college campuses, and the flapper remains one of the most enduring images of the 1920s. She wore lipstick and rouge, especially after *The Saturday Evening Post* magazine, which had condemned makeup early in the 1920s, began accepting advertisements for cosmetics. She cut her hair into a short, blunt style called a bob and plucked her eyebrows. She drove cars, went to movies, and adopted such fads as playing ping-pong and mah-jongg. She drank. Hemlines rose dramatically, and new sheer stockings gave the impression of nude legs, prompting the states of Ohio and Utah to pass laws

THE FLAPPER

Many theories have been offered about the origin of the term *flapper*. One popular theory is that during the 1920s, women adopted the fashion trend of wearing unfastened boots. The word *flapper* suggested the "flap-flap" sound the boots made when their wearers walked. Others believe that it came from the sound that women's fringes, beads, and jewelry made when they danced the Charleston. Still others believe that it described the way that the new woman walked, flapping her limbs with a new, self-confident swagger rather than walking elegantly.

What is certain is that the word did not originate in America. It had been used in England since at least the 19th century. Sometimes it was used to refer to young women with boyish figures. More frequently it referred to a friendly, jolly girl or young woman who would be happy riding on the flapper bracket, or passenger seat, on a motorcycle.

In 1929, author Preston W. Slosson described the flapper: She was "breezy, slangy, and informal in manner; slim and boyish in form; covered in silk and fur that clung to her as close as onion skin; with carmined [red] lips, plucked eyebrows and close-fitting helmet of hair; gay, plucky and confident." (*The Great Crusade and After, 1914–1918*).

DANCE MARATHONS

One example of excess during the 1920s and into the 1930s was the dance marathon. In a dance marathon, couples danced continuously for a long period of time until one couple outlasted all the others. Usually, though, the rules specified that dancers could take brief rest periods. Generally, a dancer was not allowed to fall asleep while on the floor, but some marathons allowed one of the dancers to fall asleep as long as the other kept the person standing and in motion. Many of these marathons lasted for days, even weeks. The longest-running dance marathon lasted for just over 157 days. Dancers competed for prize money, but some were professional entertainers who were seeking publicity. Some were placed in the contest to stage fights or provide some other type of preplanned entertainment to draw attention.

Dance marathons seem today like a harmless fad, but in fact some people actually died during them. Others suffered lasting injuries. For this reason, most states eventually outlawed dance marathons.

Holeproof Hosiery

Changes in women's fashion, especially higher hemlines, created a need for hosiery; many Americans found the impression of nude legs shocking. *(Private Collection)*

fixing hem lengths at no more than seven inches above the floor. Fashions were lightweight and comfortable. Some women adopted an exotic, ancient Egyptian style in the wake of excitement over the discovery of King Tutankhamen's lavish tomb in Egypt in 1922. ("King Tut" was the Egyptian pharoah who ruled from 1333 to 1323 B.C.) The restrictive corset (a tight undergarment) became a thing of the past. The sexual liberation of women took a first step when birth-control advocate Margaret Sanger opened the first birth-control clinics, in New York City during the 1920s.

To the generation reared during the Victorian age of the 19th century, the world of the 1920s must have seemed topsy-turvy at best. At worst, it seemed headed to moral ruin. Either way, American photojournalists were there to document what they often saw as the antics of the flapper. Magazines printed pictures of women wearing scandalous one-piece bathing suits to

President Warren Harding's pet dog was named Laddie Boy. *(Library of Congress)*

One of Florence Harding's close friends was Fanny Brice, a popular singer and entertainer immortalized in Barbra Streisand's movie *Funny Girl*. Brice once told the first lady that she had plastic surgery on her nose to get it back to "normalcy." The president's mistake had stuck.

A PUZZLING FAD

Crossword puzzles were a craze in the 1920s. The first books of crossword puzzles, published by Simon & Schuster, even came with a pencil helpfully attached. One woman filed for divorce because, she said, her husband's obsession with crosswords made her a "crossword widow."

the beach, dancing the Charleston while wearing raccoon coats on New York City's Fifth Avenue, or collapsing in exhaustion after dance marathons that often lasted days or even weeks. Magazines even printed pictures of women smoking— and in public (sales of cigarettes increased from about 15 billion before the war to more than 100 billion in 1928 as more women began smoking). They chronicled the thoroughly modern young woman's newfound leisure provided by economic growth and laborsaving appliances. She lounged in bright, colorful costumes while at a jazz club, working a crossword puzzle (first published in newspapers in 1924), or reading one of the many new magazines launched during the 1920s. These included *Reader's Digest* (1922), *Time* (1923), and *The New Yorker* (1925), which billed itself as the magazine for "caviar sophisticates . . . not for the old lady in

MAH-JONGG

Mah-jongg, sometimes spelled Mah jong or majongh, originated in China in the 19th century. It continues to be popular in China and Japan as well as the United States. It is usually played with tiles, though it can also be played with cards. Along with the mania associated with King Tut, it reflected the 1920s interest in things exotic and faraway.

A mah-jongg set consists of 144 tiles:

• Three suits with tiles numbered 1 to 9. The English names for the suits are circles, bamboos, and characters. There are four identical copies of each suit tile, or 108 suit tiles in all.

• The four directions or winds (east, north, west, south); there are four copies of each for a total of 16 tiles.

• Three colors or dragons (red, green, white); again, there are four copies of each, for a total of 12 tiles.

• Bonus tiles: Usually these include four different flower tiles and four different season tiles.

Generally, 13 tiles are dealt to each player. The object is, by drawing and discarding, to form a winning hand of 14 tiles, normally four sets of three and a pair. A set of three can be three identical tiles or three tiles of the same suit in numerical sequence. The game can also be won with various special hands containing other combinations of tiles. Extra bonuses can be won for feats such as winning with a single suit or a hand consisting entirely of winds and dragons.

Many American artists and writers settled in Paris in the 1920s. *(Library of Congress)*

Dubuque [Iowa]." The standard for trendy women was set by such film idols as Greta Garbo and Clara Bow, whose pictures filled the fan magazines that were growing in popularity.

Many women's rights activists, though, were disappointed that the Nineteenth Amendment did not lead to changes in the role of women. During the 1920s, employment of women increased by only about 1 percent. Women were still employed largely in lower-paying service jobs; the number of women doctors actually decreased during the decade. Men remained the main breadwinners, and women still took care of children and the home. Most popular magazines supported this state of affairs.

The Book-of-the-Month Club was formed in 1926 to satisfy the growing demand for popular literature.

American writer Gertrude Stein was at the center of a community of artists and writers living in Paris during the 1920s. *(Library of Congress)*

Partly under Harding's influence, the number of golf courses in the United States, fewer than 2,000 in 1920, more than tripled during the 1920s. In 1920 there were about 5,000 bowling teams; by 1930 there were 40,000.

LITERARY TRENDS IN THE 1920s: THE LOST GENERATION

During the 1920s a wide gulf separated some segments of American society. This gulf could often be seen in the differing beliefs and values of the big city versus the small town. In 1920, a majority of Americans lived in small towns and rural areas. By the end of the decade, this balance had shifted so that by 1930 a slim majority of Americans lived in larger towns and big cities. Artists, intellectuals, and sophisticated people who considered themselves to be modern tended to gravitate toward the big cities. They often felt that the small towns and rural areas of the Midwest and South were wastelands. They saw themselves as modern and progressive but often believed small-town rural folk to be bigoted and hopelessly out-of-date. For their part, small-town and rural Americans, especially those who held traditional religious beliefs, tended to see the modern culture of the cities as shocking and immoral. To them, the flapper and the speakeasy, drinking and dance marathons, foreigners and socialists represented all that was wrong with the United States at the time.

This division was often reflected at the voting booth, with rural and small-town voters usually favoring conservative candidates. But a similar division could more and more be found in the decade's art, literature, and entertainment. Ordinary folk—the working classes and many members of the middle class—tended to prefer more mass-pleasing forms of entertainment. These included sports, magic acts, elaborate stage shows such as *The Ziegfeld Follies,* vaudeville (onstage variety shows consisting of dance, music, and comedy sketches), and, increasingly, movies. In contrast, the more modern, intellectual set tended to be less interested in popular entertainment. To them, the purpose of art and literature was to take a critical look at U.S. culture, history, and society. People with this attitude were often called highbrows.

"BERNICE BOBS HER HAIR"

F. Scott Fitzgerald's short story "Bernice Bobs Her Hair" was published in *The Saturday Evening Post* on May 1, 1920. It tells the story of Bernice, a shy young woman who leaves the safety of home to visit her flapper cousin Marjorie. Marjorie tries to teach Bernice how to be more modern and adopt more of a flapper image.

Bernice stood on the curb and looked at the sign, Sevier Barber-Shop. It was a guillotine indeed, and the hangman was the first barber, who, attired in a white coat and smoking a cigarette, leaned nonchalantly against the first chair…Would they blindfold her? No, but they would tie a white cloth round her neck lest any of her blood—nonsense—hair-should get on her clothes…

With her chin in the air she crossed the sidewalk, pushed open the swinging screen-door, and giving not a glance to the uproarious, riotous row that occupied the waiting bench, went up to the first barber.

"I want you to bob my hair."

The first barber's mouth slid somewhat open. His cigarette dropped to the floor.

"Huh?"

"My hair—bob it!"…

Twenty minutes later the barber swung her round to face the mirror, and she flinched at the full extent of the damage that had been wrought. Her hair was not curly, and now it lay in lank lifeless blocks on both sides of her suddenly pale face. It was ugly as sin—she had known it would be ugly as sin. Her face's chief charm had been a Madonna-like simplicity. Now that was gone and she was—well, frightfully mediocre—not stagy; only ridiculous, like a Greenwich Villager who had left her spectacles at home.

Many of the most well-known highbrow writers of the 1920s are referred to as members of the Lost Generation. This phrase originated with Gertrude Stein (1874–1946), an American writer who spent most of her adult life living and writing in France. Stein left the United States in 1903 because she believed that she could find more artistic and personal freedom in Europe, away from what she saw as the restrictions of American life.

AMERICAN EXPATRIATE WRITERS

After World War I, Gertrude Stein was the central figure in a community of American expatriate writers in Paris. (An expatriate is a citizen of one country who chooses to live in another.) Some of these writers had driven ambulances in France or Italy during the early years of the war; others had fought after the United States entered the war in 1917. Among the many writers in this group of

American writer Ernest Hemingway married his first wife, Hadley Richardson of Chicago, in September 1921. *(JFK Presidential Library)*

The novels of Theodore Dreiser, especially *An American Tragedy,* critiqued the American emphasis on financial success. *(Private Collection)*

One of America's greatest novelists and short story writers, William Faulkner, published his first novels in the 1920s. *(Private Collection)*

expatriate Americans were Ernest Hemingway and F. Scott Fitzgerald, who both wrote novels and short stories, and poet e. e. cummings. Many African-American writers, including Richard Wright, as well as jazz artists found Europe a more inviting place, free from some of America's racial prejudices.

These writers had been greatly disillusioned by the brutality and slaughter of the war, and their work influenced a whole generation of writers. They distrusted idealism and American traditions. They saw the mass of postwar Americans as moralistic, vulgar, and devoted to business and making money. In contrast, they saw Europe as more refined and culturally sophisticated. There they could devote themselves to art and ideas. There was no Prohibition, and people who held radical political ideas were accepted. Their rootlessness caused Gertrude Stein to tell Hemingway that his was a "lost generation."

An example of the type of work produced by this generation of writers is *A Farewell to Arms* by Ernest Hemingway (1899–1961). This 1929 novel tells the story of Frederick Henry, an ambulance driver injured in Italy during World War I. He falls in love with the English nurse, Catherine Barkley, who tends his wounds. She becomes pregnant but refuses to marry him, so he returns to his military unit. Later, the Italian army collapses and retreats, so Henry deserts. He is reunited with Catherine, and the two flee to Switzerland, where their life together ends. The novel captures the feeling of desolation and homelessness felt by many young Americans in the years after the war.

THE BOHEMIAN SET

Not all American writers, of course, left for Europe. Many settled in places such as New York City's Greenwich Village, which offered an atmosphere similar to that of Paris. Like Paris and other European capitals, Greenwich Village was inexpensive and sociable. Penniless writers and artists joined together to reject the values of American society at large and devote themselves to art and literature. They published much of their work in small literary magazines that mocked traditional social restraints and the modern obsession with making money. Their emphasis was on self-expression, without paying attention to the standards of traditional politeness. During these years, the work of Austrian psychologist Sigmund Freud (1856–1939) was much in vogue. They adopted his language, calling conventional people "repressed" and "maladjusted." They valued sincerity and beauty. They believed that women should enjoy the same rights as men, so women smoked, drank, and pursued love rather than marriage. One of the leading figures in this set was the poet Edna St. Vincent Millay. Millay (1892–1950) left her home in Maine to settle in Greenwich Village for a time. In addition to writing poetry, she wrote plays and acted onstage. Perhaps her most famous line, from her 1920 poetry collection entitled *A Few Figs and Thistles,* was "My candle burns at both ends." Many young writers, some of whom referred to themselves as flaming youth, took up this line as their watchword.

Much 1920s literature had a common theme, whether it was written by a New York City bohemian, an expatriate in Paris, or a writer living a more conventional life: rejection of American culture as crass and materialistic. At least three now-classic books develop this theme, but it can be found in many others. One is *This Side of Paradise,* a 1920 novel by F. Scott Fitzgerald (1896–1940). The handsome, reckless Fitzgerald seemed ideally suited to provide snapshots of the Roaring Twenties, which he called "the greatest, gaudiest spree in history." He spent the decade in Paris, where he struggled to make enough money to support a lavish lifestyle (in contrast to many other American writers living

STEARNS'S WORDS
One American expatriate who expressed his views about American culture was Harold Stearns. Stearns is not widely read today, but he stated the expatriate attitude clearly in a 1921 essay collection entitled *America and the Young Intellectual.* He wrote that a person of his generation "does dislike, almost to the point of hatred and certainly to the point of contempt, the type of people who dominate in our civilization."

The word *bohemian* comes from Bohemia, a region in what is now the Czech Republic where gypsies and wanderers tended to gather. Today it is still used to refer to any colony of artists and intellectuals who give up financial success to pursue art and ideas.

Edna St. Vincent Millay was a leading poet in the Greenwich Village, New York, set during the 1920s. *(Private Collection)*

WHAT PRICE GLORY?

One of the most popular Broadway (New York) plays of the 1920s was *What Price Glory?* (1924) by Maxwell Anderson and Laurence Stallings. Although it was light-hearted, the play questioned patriotic views of World War I and was shocking because the soldier-characters used realistic profanity. The final line spoken by one of the main characters expressed a viewpoint about the war that many Americans had adopted: "What a lot of God damn fools it takes to make a war!"

there), often by writing short stories for such magazines as *The Saturday Evening Post. This Side of Paradise,* his first novel, revealed the new morality of young people in the Roaring Twenties and set the tone for the decade. It tells the story of Amory Blaine, an affluent, spoiled college student whose efforts to find love are corrupted by his greed and materialism. It glorifies an irresponsible life of pleasure. More than a few of its readers shared Blaine's belief that he had "grown up to find all Gods dead, all wars fought, all faiths in man shaken."

A second influential novel is *Babbitt,* written in 1922 by Sinclair Lewis (1885–1951). The novel tells the story of George Babbitt, a prosperous real estate broker in a fictional midwestern town called Zenith. Babbitt is a town booster and a pillar of the Zenith business community. He briefly—but only briefly—questions his middle-class values after his best friend is arrested for shooting his own wife. The novel is a sharp satire on American middle-class life. The word *Babbittry* became a synonym for thoughtless conformity, hypocrisy, and materialism. It is little accident that the book was published during the administration of President Warren G. Harding. Many readers thought that Babbitt could almost serve as a portrait of the contented, probusiness people who supported Harding.

The third is *An American Tragedy,* a 1925 novel by Theodore Dreiser (1871–1945). The central character of the novel is Clyde Griffiths, a young man from a poor background who achieves some success. Griffiths, though, despite his religious upbringing, is a despicable character, a social climber driven by greed. He is so desperate for money and position that he murders his poor fiancée so that he can pursue a wealthy socialite. In the end, he is tried, convicted, and executed for the murder. The novel strongly condemns materialism and the American dream of financial success.

Many writers did not achieve popular success at the time. Ernest Hemingway, now considered a major

THE ZIEGFELD FOLLIES

The Ziegfeld Follies was the brainchild of Florenz ("Flo") Ziegfeld (ca. 1867–1932), one of the great showmen of the 20th century. Ziegfeld rejected his training in classical music to produce more popular forms of entertainment. In 1907, two stage producers asked him to develop a light musical show to put on during the slow summer theater season. The result was *The Follies of 1907.* The show was so successful that Ziegfeld produced a version of it each year, eventually renaming it *The Ziegfeld Follies.*

The Ziegfeld Follies reached the height of its popularity in the 1920s. The show was a lavish, spectacular presentation, combining music, dance, and sketch comedy in 23 scenes over two acts. The costumes of the performers were elaborate and showy; the scenery was innovative. The *Follies'* most notable fea-

ture was the chorus, which featured 60 beautiful women. Many big names in entertainment—singers Fanny Brice and Eddie Cantor, comedians Will Rogers and W. C. Fields—became stars after performing in the *Follies.* Opening-night productions were always attended by the business and social elite, including the Rockefellers, the Vanderbilts, the Guggenheims, and show-business personalities.

Ziegfeld was married to Billie Burke, the actress who played Glinda, the Good Witch, in the famous 1939 film *The Wizard of Oz.*

Vaudeville shows were a popular form of entertainment in the early 1920s, and Flo Ziegfeld gained fame as a popular vaudeville director. *(Library of Congress)*

American writer, did not have a best seller until 1940. More popular authors included Zane Grey, who had a western novel on the best-seller list every year from 1917 to 1925: *The U.P. Trail, The Mysterious Rider, The Wanderer of the Wasteland, The Call of the Canyon,* and others. Another best-selling author was Edna Ferber, whose work is memorable for its strong heroines. Her novel *So Big* won the Pulitzer Prize, a prestigious literary award, in 1924, and *Show Boat,* published in 1926, was turned into a popular musical play.

Also during the 1920s, William Faulkner (1897–1962), regarded by some critics as America's greatest writer, got his start. He published his first novel, *Soldier's Pay,* in 1926. Then in 1929 he published *Sartoris,* his first major novel about a fictional county in Mississippi. *Sartoris* and most of Faulkner's

THE BIG APPLE
New York City is often called the Big Apple. The expression was first used in the 1920s by sports stars and entertainment figures, especially jazz musicians. They used it to say "I've hit the big time, I'm playing in New York City, I've reached the big apple at the top of the tree of success." African-American writer Alain Locke used the now well-known phrase in 1919 when he called Harlem "the precious fruit in the Garden of Eden, the big apple."

FORE! OR PLUS FOURS

Changes in fashion were not restricted to women—though generally men dressed more conservatively than women during the decade. One fashion rage among young men was "plus fours." These were especially baggy knickers (short pants) that were called plus fours because they were made with an additional four inches of material. They were widely worn by men as sportswear during activities such as golf during the 1920s and 1930s. The style was popularized by the British Prince of Wales.

numerous other novels and short stories explore the Old South as it struggled to cling to old values while adapting to modern life after the Civil War.

In nonfiction, one of the most popular books of the decade was written by a French writer named Emile Coué. Published in English in 1922, the book, *Self-Mastery Through Conscious Auto-Suggestion,* was a sensation. Coué Institutes were founded, and Coué himself was highly popular on the lecture circuit. Millions of Americans could often be heard repeating Coué's slogan: "Every day in every way I am getting better and better." The book, and the slogan, captured the sense of optimism about the future among many Americans during the Roaring Twenties. One way that many middle-class Americans tried to "get better and better" was by reading, and following, Emily Post's best-selling 1923 book, *Etiquette.*

Americans' optimistic belief in self-improvement fueled the sale of a number of popular books. Guests could apply what they learned about etiquette at dinner parties where the hostess followed recipes from Fannie Farmer's *The Boston Cooking School Cook Book,* which held a firm place on the best-seller lists from 1924 through 1926. Those trying to slim down to a boyish figure could read Lulu Hunt Peters's *Diet and Health,* which was a best seller for four years running from 1922 to 1926.

The 1920s began as a decade of contrasts and tensions between the idealism of Woodrow Wilson and the practicality of Warren Harding, between highbrow culture and lowbrow entertainment, between big-city sophistication and small-town and rural traditions, between belief in the promise of America and rejection of American values.

CHAPTER 3

THE HARDING YEARS, 1921–1923

President Warren G. Harding addresses the U.S. House of Representatives. *(Library of Congress)*

PRESIDENT WARREN G. HARDING inherited from the Wilson administration an economy that was in poor condition. The Great War was the culprit. During the war, the government had closely regulated the economy to increase production and efficiency. As an example, the government took over the operation of the railroads to make sure that they were contributing to the war effort in moving troops, raw materials, and finished goods. Americans had pitched in because they believed that government regulation was needed during wartime. But when the war ended, the government had made no clear plans

"We want less government in business and more business in government."

—President Warren Harding

A strike leader addresses a crowd in Gary, Indiana, in 1919. *(Library of Congress)*

HOLY WATER?

Under Prohibition, alcohol could be sold if it was to be used as sacramental wine in churches and synagogues. The nation witnessed a rash of people who claimed to be ministers and rabbis and wanting to buy sacramental wine for congregations whose numbers they hugely inflated. More than one New Yorker claiming to be a Jewish rabbi tried to buy wine for congregations that were larger than the entire Jewish population of the city.

for demobilization (shifting to a peacetime economy). Abruptly, all the controls were removed. Millions of soldiers suddenly returned to the job market. Government contracts for war materials were canceled. The nation, in President Wilson's words, "took the harness off" too quickly.

In the short run, business had boomed. During the war, few products were available for Americans to spend their money on. So immediately after the war, they spent their money on cars, housing, and other goods that had been in short supply. Industry expanded and hired more workers to produce products to meet the rising demand, so unemployment of returning soldiers was not an immediate problem. Because of increased demand, some goods were in short supply, so prices went up. This inflation—a general increase in the price of goods—raised the cost of living. This increase in the cost of living caused labor unrest. Labor unions, which had won wage increases during the war, fought for yet higher wages to keep up with rising prices. In 1919 and 1920, labor strikes became commonplace. These strikes caused more shortages, further increasing prices, and in turn creating yet more labor unrest.

THE ECONOMIC DOWNTURN

The result of this spiral was a sharp economic downturn between 1920 and the summer of 1922. In 1920, the U.S. gross domestic product—the total value of goods and services produced in the country—was $88.9 billion. In both 1921 and 1922, that figure dropped to $74 billion. In 1920, the total gross income (the amount of money taken in) of U.S. corporations was about $118 billion. In 1921, that number dropped to $91 billion, although it recovered to almost $101 billion in 1922. These and other numbers showed that overall the economy was shrinking, not growing.

Harding believed that the best way to turn the economy around was for the government to be more probusiness. To help bring the nation out of its economic doldrums, in 1921 he appointed a businessman, Andrew W. Mellon (1855–1937), as secretary of the Treasury. Mellon was a well-known financier and industrialist. He had amassed a fortune in banking and was a major shareholder in such important companies as the Aluminum Company of America and the Gulf Oil Corporation. Late in his career, though, he decided he had no need for further wealth. He wanted to apply his business skills in government, and he had strong opinions about how government should be run. He believed that government should be operated more like a business. Mellon was horrified that the federal government did not prepare a single budget for all of its operations. Instead, budgeting was done on a department-by-department basis. Mellon changed that.

As secretary of the Treasury, Mellon was the dominant figure in the Harding administration. He made policy proposals that even the president admitted he did not understand. Under Mellon's leadership, high taxes on the wealthy were cut. So were taxes on corporate income, which had been high to finance the war effort. These tax cuts stimulated more investment in business. He also reduced the national debt by cutting government spending. In 1920, the budget for the federal government was $6.4 billion. By 1922 he had brought that number down to $3.3 billion. (Mellon continued as treasury secretary under the next president, Calvin Coolidge, and by 1927 he had reduced the federal budget to $2.9 billion.) He also proposed raising tariffs,

Secretary of the Treasury Andrew W. Mellon was one of the most dominant figures in the Harding administration. *(Library of Congress)*

Andrew W. Mellon served three consecutive administrations as secretary of the Treasury. He was appointed by Harding and took office March 4, 1921. Mellon served presidents Harding, Coolidge, and Hoover until February 12, 1932.

Eugene V. Debs was a socialist labor leader who was imprisoned for speaking out against World War I and urging resistance to the military draft. *(Private Collection)*

Shortly after Warren's death, Florence Harding destroyed many boxes of his papers. Some believed that she poisoned her husband, either to spare him the looming scandals or because of his womanizing. No evidence supports this accusation.

which are a form of tax on imported goods that raises their prices. Tariffs made U.S. goods relatively less expensive for Americans, increasing demand for U.S.-made products.

These policies were starting to work. Americans were buying more goods, so in 1923 the gross national product rose to $86.1 billion. Many of the products Americans were buying were durable goods—such items as cars and refrigerators (rather than nondurable goods such as food and clothing). The numbers for durable goods were looking much better. The total value of durable goods had fallen from about $4.9 billion in 1920 to about $3.27 billion in 1921. But by 1923 this number had soared to about $5.37 billion. Americans had more money, and they were looking for new products to spend it on. The 1920s were the first decade of mass consumerism in U.S. history.

AN ADMINISTRATION PLAGUED BY SCANDAL: TEAPOT DOME

The Harding administration was short, lasting just 882 days, but it managed some accomplishments. In addition to improving the economy, Harding tried to help farmers, who were suffering because of low prices. He also granted freedom to many wartime political prisoners, including socialist labor leader Eugene V. Debs. (Socialism calls for state ownership of industry and a more equal distribution of wealth.) In 1918, Debs had made a speech critical of capitalism and the war and urging resistance to the military draft. Under the Sedition Act, he was tried, convicted, and sentenced to 10 years in the federal penitentiary in Atlanta. Remarkably, as prisoner 9653, he conducted the last of several campaigns for president as the Socialist Party candidate in 1920 and actually tallied nearly a million votes.

Harding also made some sound cabinet appointments, including future president Herbert Hoover in the Commerce Department, Charles Evans Hughes as secretary of state, and Henry C. Wallace as agriculture secretary. In foreign affairs, Harding is best known for the Washington Conference, which was held in Washington, D.C., in 1921 and 1922. This conference resulted in several treaties. One was an arms treaty that limited the number of warships the United States, Britain, France, Italy, and Japan could have. While these treaties did not prevent World War II two decades later, they were at least an attempt to achieve the lasting peace that President Woodrow Wilson had sought.

Two of President Harding's best cabinet appointments were Herbert Hoover (left) as secretary of commerce and Charles Evans Hughes (right) as secretary of state. (Library of Congress)

Despite these accomplishments, historians generally regard Harding as among the worst U.S. presidents—if not *the* worst. Although he was hardworking, he was temperamentally unsuited to high office. He often failed to pay attention to what members of his administration were doing. He was too trusting, especially of his political friends. Many of these friends are often referred to as the Ohio Gang or the Ohio Cronies because they were friends from Ohio he appointed to office only because he liked them, not because of their qualifications. He often invited them to the White House for poker and bootleg whiskey.

Many of the Ohio Gang were corrupt. If Harding's presidency was a failure, it was largely because of the many scandals in which these men were involved. The head of the Veterans Bureau, Charles Forbes, stole $200 million intended for the construction of veterans' hospitals. He also resold government-owned hospital supplies to his friends as surplus, usually for pennies on the dollar. Harding's attorney general, Harry Daugherty, stole German bank deposits that the U.S. government

FALLING PRICES

During the 1920s, farmers' share of national income fell by 50 percent. One reason was that as farming recovered in postwar Europe, European farm output was competing against American output. This came at a time when American farm output was increasing because of the use of fertilizers and more modern machinery. This increase in production forced prices down even further.

had seized during World War I. This money was supposed to be returned to its German owners, but much of it found its way into Daugherty's pockets. In a criminal trial, Daugherty escaped conviction probably by bribing jury members. When asked by a journalist whether he was unfairly accused or a clever crook, Daugherty smiled and said, "You can take your pick." Daugherty's associate, Jess Smith, exchanged political favors for bribes. Under Prohibition, liquor could be purchased from government warehouses if it was for use in making medicines. The merchant, though, had to have a special permit from the government. Smith took bribes to award these liquor permits to bootleggers.

The most infamous scandal of the Harding years was Teapot Dome. At the center of it was Harding's secretary of the interior, Albert Fall (1861–1944). Fall had led a colorful life. He was born in Kentucky, but he spent much of his life in the West. After working as a

President Harding (third from the right) is pictured with his cabinet; Albert Fall, the disgraced secretary of the interior, is standing next to the president in the front row, third from the left. *(Library of Congress)*

lumberjack and miner, he became a U.S. marshal in Texas. He once disarmed an Old West gunslinger in an El Paso saloon. Later he bought a newspaper business and ran for local office. During the campaign, Fall and a group of cowboys got into a gunfight with the local sheriff in Las Cruces, New Mexico.

Fall was a U.S. senator in 1915 when Harding arrived at the Capitol to take his own Senate seat. On the Senate floor, Fall occupied the desk next to Harding's, and he showed Harding the political ropes in Washington. Harding was charmed by Fall, who wore a big Stetson hat and gambler's bow tie. The two often played poker together. So when Harding was elected president, he appointed Hall secretary of the interior.

At this time, the U.S. government owned a number of oil reserves. One was located in Elk Hills, California. Another was located beneath Teapot Dome, a dome-shaped sandstone formation in Wyoming. These and other oil reserves were held for the future use of the navy, which needed a reliable source of oil. Fall, though, persuaded the secretary of the navy to transfer the properties to the control of the Department of the Interior. Fall then leased these properties to private oil companies, which drilled the sites and sold the oil. Critics protested, but Fall argued that the properties had to be drilled because the oil beneath them was being drained off by neighboring drillers. The U.S. Senate, though, was not convinced. It ordered a full-scale investigation of the circumstances surrounding the leases.

Conducting the investigation was Thomas Walsh, a senator from Montana. Walsh pushed harder in the investigation after his office was ransacked, his phone was tapped, and his daughter was threatened. He soon discovered that Fall had accepted a so-called loan of $100,000 in cash from Edward Doheny, owner of the company that leased the Elk Hills property and a friend from Fall's early days. Doheny later testified that he expected to make more than $100 million from the Elk

The administration of the nation's 29th president, Warren G. Harding, was marred by scandal. *(Library of Congress)*

In 1921, the year President Harding took office, the average hourly wage of a factory worker was about 51 cents. On average, factory workers worked 43 hours a week, so their average weekly earnings were $22.18. In 1922 that weekly figure fell to $21.51.

A DISTINGUISHED CAREER

Charles Evans Hughes (1862–1948) served as governor of New York and as a U.S. Supreme Court justice. Herbert Hoover appointed him chief justice of the Supreme Court in 1930. In 1916 he had lost the presidency to Woodrow Wilson by fewer than 600,000 votes.

> Comedian Will Rogers expressed his belief in the hypocrisy of American values when he said that Americans would continue to vote dry (in favor of Prohibition) as long as they could stagger to the polls.

Hill property. Fall also took more than $300,000 from another friend, Harry Sinclair, who owned the company that leased the Teapot Dome reserve. Sinclair actually made $25 million from the property. These payments to Fall, it turned out, were bribes.

In 1929, Fall went to trial and was convicted for accepting a bribe. He was fined $100,000. He also served one year in prison, the first cabinet officer ever to be jailed for crimes committed while in office. Until his death, Fall maintained that he had not been bribed. He also insisted that the money the government earned from the leases was used to build oil storage tanks that helped the U.S. military survive the attack on Pearl Harbor in 1941. Few people believed him, and many

President Harding's secretary of state, Charles Evans Hughes, is shown with his wife and daughter. *(Library of Congress)*

Americans came to believe that the U.S. government had been for sale during Harding's term in office. *Teapot Dome* became part of the language, a synonym for corruption in government.

Most of this corruption was revealed after Harding's death. While he was still alive, though, the president had inklings that his friends were betraying him. In June 1923, his spirits were low and his health was poor. He had long suffered from high blood pressure. He left Washington to go on a speaking tour in the West, including Alaska. On his return from Alaska in late July, he came down with what at first appeared to be ptomaine poisoning, a form of food poisoning, but was in fact a heart attack. He died in San Francisco on August 2.

Americans deeply mourned Harding's death, but as evidence of the scandals began to come out, their sadness turned to scorn. That scorn deepened in 1927 after Harding's mistress Nan Britton published a best-selling book called *The President's Daughter*. In this book, Britton provided sordid details of a long love affair with the president. She claimed that the Secret Service regularly smuggled her into the White House to see him. She also claimed that in 1919 she had given birth to a daughter fathered by the president. Other women claimed that they, too, had affairs with the president. All of these revelations forever tarnished the reputation of Warren G. Harding, a sincere, otherwise well-meaning man who wanted to be a good president but did not quite know how.

RACE RELATIONS DURING THE HARDING PRESIDENCY AND BEYOND

During Warren Harding's campaign for the presidency, a pamphlet was widely circulated by a small group of his political opponents. The pamphlet, entitled *Shadow of Blooming Grove*, claimed that Harding had "Negro" ancestors. Some of Harding's opponents believed that

FLAGPOLE SITTERS

The 1920s witnessed the birth of modern advertising. Businesses devised a number of gimmicks to draw attention to their stores. One of the most popular was flagpole sitting. In 1924 Alvin "Shipwreck" Kelly, who once sat atop a flagpole in Baltimore for 23 days and 7 hours, started the fad. In all, Kelly spent 20,163 hours atop flagpoles for various businesses across the country.

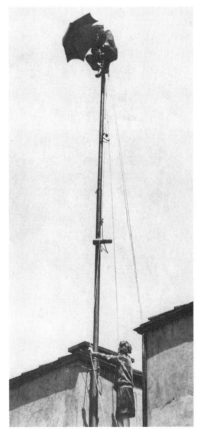

Flagpole sitting as a form of advertising for a business became a popular fad during the 1920s. *(Private Collection)*

The Ku Klux Klan, led in 1926 by "imperial wizard" H. W. Evans, attracted many new members during the 1920s. *(Library of Congress)*

this information would discredit him. Their viewpoint suggests that race divisions continued to infect American society throughout the 1920s.

Many Americans in the 1920s wanted to see a fairer, more open society. They opposed discrimination against African Americans. Their efforts were thwarted by others who wanted to keep African Americans in an inferior position. Prominent among this group was the newly reborn Ku Klux Klan (KKK).

THE RESURGENCE OF THE KU KLUX KLAN AND LYNCHINGS

The KKK, an organization whose name is still synonymous with racial hatred, was born in 1866 in Tennessee. During its early years, it was limited primarily to the rural south. The purpose of the Klan was to oppose Reconstruction after the Civil War and to deny newly freed African Americans their civil rights. (Reconstruction refers to the laws that were designed to reform the Southern states that had left, or seceded, from the Union during the war.) The power of the Klan ebbed after the federal government began to arrest and try Klan members who were guilty of violence against blacks and even against whites who supported Reconstruction.

The Klan, though, did not disappear. It was reborn in 1915, in part as a result of D. W. Griffith's now-classic film *The Birth of a Nation*. This popular movie, based on a 1905 book called *The Clansman* by Thomas Dixon, romanticized the Klan. It depicted its members as noble defenders of decency, of a white, Protestant way of life; it depicted blacks as drunkards, rapists, and a threat to that way of life. To this day, film historians are torn between admiration for the film's technical brilliance and disgust at its despicable message. Further encouraging the resurgence of the Klan was the superpatriotism of the Great War, World War I, when anyone who was not white, Protestant, and American was suspect.

In its heyday in the early 1920s, the new Klan attracted at least 3 million members; some estimates are as high as 4.5 million. Unlike the old Klan, the new Klan attracted members outside the south and in cities. It backed the election of public officials in Oklahoma, Indiana, Oregon, and other states. While most of its members were lower middle class, some were leaders in their communities. Like the old Klan, the new Klan relied on intimidation to suppress any group that it saw as a threat.

The new Klan fed on a number of fears. These included fear of African Americans, who were moving into northern American cities in greater numbers during the so-called Great Migration. During the 1920s, up to a million southern blacks relocated, in part to escape the racism in the rural South, in part to find jobs in the industrialized cities of the North and Midwest. This migration had actually begun earlier. The black population of Chicago, for example, had grown from about 44,000 in 1910 to 110,000 in 1920. During the 1920s, the process accelerated. The black population of Harlem, New York, grew from 50,000 in 1914 to 165,000 in 1930. Similar growth took place in other cities, such as Detroit and Cleveland.

The experience of most of these migrants was bitter. Labor unions continued to refuse to admit African Americans, so wages in the black community remained low. At the same time, housing shortages, caused by the influx of people, led to increases in rents, which doubled in Harlem between 1919 and 1927. The result was the formation of urban ghettoes marked by disease, poverty, high infant mortality, crime, and other social ills. Nonetheless, the Klan and its sympathizers believed that African Americans were depriving white people of jobs.

> *"So many people of my age, we were born in the North, but our roots were southern because of our parents, the peers of our parents, our customs, mores, were all southern."*
>
> —Painter Jacob Lawrence, discussing his paintings of the Great Migration

RESISTANCE TO THE KKK

Many Americans resisted the spread of the KKK. One was William Allen White, a nationally famous journalist from Kansas. In a letter to the editor of the *New York World* dated September 17, 1921, White commented on the resistance the Klan met in Emporia, Kansas.

An organizer of the Ku Klux Klan was in Emporia the other day, and the men whom he invited to join his band at $10 per join turned him down.

> *Anti-foreigners*
> *Anti-Catholics*
> *Anti-Negroes.*

There are, of course, bad foreigners and good ones, good Catholics and bad ones, and all kinds of Negroes. To make a case against a birthplace, a religion, or a race is wickedly un-American and cowardly. The whole trouble with the Ku Klux Klan is that it is based upon such deep foolishness that it is bound to be a menace to good government in any community. Any man fool enough to be Imperial Wizard would have power without responsibility and both without any sense. That is social dynamite.

For a self-constituted body of moral idiots, who would substitute the findings of the Ku Klux Klan for the processes of law to try to better conditions, would be a most un-American outrage which every good citizen should resent.

It is to the everlasting credit of Emporia that the organizer found no suckers with $10 each to squander here. Whatever Emporia may be other-wise, it believes in law and order, and absolute freedom under the Constitution for every man, no matter what birth or creed or race, to speak and meet and talk and act as a free, law-abiding citizen. The picayunish cowardice of a man who would substitute Klan rule and mob law for what our American fathers have died to establish and maintain should prove what a cheap...outfit the Klan is.

The Ku Klux Klan often used airplanes to scatter leaflets advocating its views. *(Library of Congress)*

But the Klan fed on other fears as well: of Jews and Catholics, whose social position was rising; of immigrants, who were changing the ethnic makeup of America; of radicals who called for the overthrow of the U.S. government and capitalism; and of labor unions, who were demanding a fairer share of the nation's wealth. This second Klan movement began to collapse, though, in 1925. That year, the national organizer of the Klan, the high-living David Stephenson of Indiana, was tried and convicted of a brutal murder. During his trial, Stephenson exposed the corruption of the Klan, and many members drifted away. The Klan recovered briefly in 1928 when the Democratic Party nominated Al Smith, a Catholic, to run for president, and anti-Catholic feeling ran high, but the Klan's power waned after that.

One way that some whites, especially in the rural South, attempted to suppress blacks was by lynching. *Lynching* refers to mob violence against someone thought to have broken a law or even just to have violated local customs. Usually the victim was hanged, but often the mob tortured, burned, or mutilated the victim as well. Historically, African Americans have been the main victims of lynching. Between 1882 (when records were first kept) and 1968, more than 3,400 African Americans were lynched, primarily in Mississippi, Georgia, Texas, Louisiana, and Alabama. Between 1918 and 1927, at least 417 were lynched, but this number includes only known cases. The true number is doubtless much higher. Some lynching victims in 1919 were African Americans who were still wearing their World War I military uniforms. Many of these lynchings were a response to race riots that scarred American cities in the years immediately following the war.

Lynchings are often thought of as spontaneous outbreaks of mob violence, but in fact many lynchings were planned. Local newspapers would announce them in advance; agents sold train tickets to the site of the lynching; families, including children, packed picnic lunches and turned out by the hundreds to watch the gruesome events. Often they took home souvenirs, including body parts. Many people urged the federal government to pass laws against lynching. In 1922 the House of Representatives passed such a bill, but it failed in the Senate. Although President Harding spoke out against lynching, he did not back the bill. Fortunately, the number

The name *Ku Klux Klan* was derived from a Greek word *kuklos*, meaning "circle" or "band."

RACIAL THEORIES

Even in the 1920s, many prominent writers and thinkers were opposing the concept of race as a way of dividing people in America. One of those was Franz Boas, a prominent anthropologist. In 1921 he published an essay in the *Yale Review* entitled "The Problem of the American Negro." In this essay, Boas argued that "there is neither a biological nor a psychological justification for the popular belief in the inferiority of the Negro race." He went on to say:

the social basis of the race prejudice in America is not difficult to understand. The prejudice is founded essentially on the tendency of the human mind to merge the individual in the class to which he belongs and to ascribe to him all the characteristics of his class. It does not even require a marked difference in type, such as we find when we compare Negro and white, to provoke the spirit that prevents us from recognizing individuals and compels us to see only representatives of a class endowed with imaginary qualities that we ascribe to the group as a whole. We find this spirit at work in anti-Semitism as well as in American nativism, and in the conflict between labor and capitalism. We have recently seen it at its height in the emotions called forth by a world war.

of lynchings began to drop in the 1920s and into the 1930s, in part through the efforts of the Association of Southern Women for the Prevention of Lynching.

MARCUS GARVEY: THE BLACK MOSES

In 1922, during the Harding administration, Marcus Garvey (1887–1940) was arrested and charged with mail fraud. This was a noteworthy event, for Garvey was one of the most prominent black leaders, including writers, artists, and intellectuals, who spoke out against racial injustice during the 1920s. Garvey's influence began to wane after his arrest. His ideas, though, survive and were resurrected by black leaders in the 1960s.

Garvey, often referred to as the Black Moses, was an advocate of black nationalism. That is, he wanted

Reconstruction is the term used to refer to the reorganization and reestablishment of the states that seceded from the Union during the Civil War.

to unite the black community throughout the world and make it self-reliant. He believed that only by acquiring power could the black community assert itself and be heard. To this end, he published the newspaper *Negro World* and formed the Universal Negro Improvement Association. In the early 1920s this organization had up to a million members and was the largest black nonreligious organization in African-American history.

The portly Garvey was a color-ful and outspoken leader. He usually wore a British-style military uniform, and he organized parades and pag-eants that were meant to create black pride and be a show of strength. He rejected other black organizations that sought cooperation with whites. He thought that integration was a delusion, even an insult to blacks. His movement was based largely in cities. There, blacks were concentrated in large numbers, in contrast to the isolation of the rural South. The black cultural renais-sance in Harlem and the emergence of black artistic expression such as jazz fueled his movement.

One way Garvey tried to promote black self-reliance was through business enterprises. His dream was a net-work of such enterprises controlled by blacks. One of Garvey's businesses was a toy company that produced black dolls for children. Another was a shipping compa-ny called the Black Star Line. He sold thousands of shares of the company at $5 each. The business, though, col-lapsed, leading to Garvey's arrest for mail fraud. Behind the arrest was J. Edgar Hoover, a Justice Department agent who in 1924 would be appointed the first director of the newly reorganized Federal Bureau of Investigation (FBI). Throughout his long career as FBI director, Hoover took special interest in many prominent African Americans

Marcus Garvey was a prominent black leader and advocate of black nationalism in the early 1920s until he was convicted of mail fraud. *(Library of Congress)*

Possibly the worst of the race riots occurred in Tulsa, Oklahoma, from May 31 to June 1, 1921. The riot left 60 African Americans and 21 whites dead and virtually destroyed the African-American community in that city.

W. E. B. DuBois was a prominent African-American author who called for self-determination for blacks. *(Library of Congress)*

Poet Langston Hughes was one of the most well-known African-American writers of the 1920s. *(Library of Congress)*

(including Martin Luther King Jr. many decades later in the 1960s). In 1923, Garvey was convicted. He was imprisoned in 1925, though in 1927 President Calvin Coolidge commuted the sentence, and Garvey was deported to his native Jamaica. When he died in London in 1940, he had been largely forgotten. But his emphasis on black pride, heritage, and culture survived.

Garvey was not the only black leader to press for self-determination for blacks. In 1919 the author W. E. B. DuBois wrote: "We are cowards and jackasses if . . . we do not marshal every ounce of our brain and brawn to fight . . . against the forces of hell in our own land." DuBois, too, believed in black nationalism, and he conducted a series of conferences to forge an international black movement. Similarly, in his book *The New Negro* (1925), Alain Locke wrote that the new black man "lays aside the status of beneficiary and ward for that of a collaborator and participant in American civilization." Despite the efforts of these and other black leaders and intellectuals, the hope of an end to segregation and discrimination was not realized.

THE HARLEM RENAISSANCE

Despite continuing racism, African-American writers and artists were creating important work in the 1920s. The center of this activity was New York City, especially the Harlem district, where the African-American population doubled during the 1920s. For this reason, the literary, artistic, and intellectual explosion in the African-American community of the 1920s and 1930s is called the Harlem Renaissance.

The Harlem Renaissance helped to create a new black identity. It was summed up by Alain Locke in *The New Negro:* "Negro life is seizing its first chances for group expression and self-determination." He saw the Harlem Renaissance as a chance for African-American writers and artists to transform "social disillusionment into race pride." In his 1922 *Book of American Negro Poetry,* James Weldon Johnson (1871–1938) captured the vitality of Harlem when he wrote that it was "the Mecca for the sightseer, the pleasure seeker, the curious, the adventurous, the . . . ambitious, and the talented of the entire Negro world."

Any list of writers associated with the Harlem Renaissance would be a lengthy one. The movement included the poet Langston Hughes (1902–67), who, like many white authors of the time, lived in Paris for a while and frequented a jazz club where the band was from Harlem. His 1926 essay "The Negro Artist and the Radical Mountain" gave definition to the Harlem Renaissance. Jean Toomer (1894–1967) wrote *Cane,* a 1923 book that dealt with African-American life in 1880s Georgia. In 1927 poet Countee Cullen (1903–46) came out with another anthology of African-American poetry, titled *Caroling Dusk.* These and other writers used experimental techniques in poetry, fiction, and drama to express the rhythm and vitality characteristic of African-American life. Their goal was to create a cultural life distinct from that of white, middle-class, industrial America.

Alain Locke (1886–1954) was the first African American to attend England's Oxford University as a prestigious Rhodes scholar. He became a kind of elder statesman and mentor for many of the younger writers of the Harlem Renaissance. His 1922 book *The New Negro* was a collection of work by writers associated with the movement.

James Weldon Johnson, the first African American to be admitted to the bar to practice law in Florida, wrote the song "Lift Every Voice and Sing," which became known as the "Negro National Anthem." *(Library of Congress)*

Writers of the Harlem Renaissance had little trouble finding white publishers. At the time, many Americans were fascinated by what they saw as the exotic world of Harlem and its vibrant street culture. As a result, books written by these writers sold well, and publishers actively sought out Harlem writers. Many African-American literary critics were concerned that any realistic depiction of the poverty of Harlem contained in this writing would set back the cause of civil rights and racial equality. They thought that much of this writing created a negative portrait of African-American life. The writers of the Harlem Renaissance, though, wanted to tell the truth and present their subject authentically.

Like their white counterparts in Greenwich Village, they saw the movement as one of self-expression and the development of a distinct culture. Many of the writers of the Harlem Renaissance were forgotten after the movement waned in the mid-1930s although the work of some of these writers, including DuBois, Hughes, Toomer, Cullen, Arna Bontemps, and others holds a secure place in the history of modern American literature and continues to influence people today. Taken as a whole, the work of the Harlem Renaissance writers offered white and black Americans a portrait of black life that was based on reality rather than on damaging and outdated stereotypes.

CHAPTER 4

THE PRESIDENCY OF CALVIN COOLIDGE, 1923–1924

WHEN PRESIDENT HARDING DIED ON August 2, 1923, his vice president, Calvin Coolidge, was vacationing at his father's farm in Plymouth Notch, Vermont. Coolidge had spent the day making hay and had been in bed for three hours when news of the president's death arrived just before midnight. By the light of a coal-oil lamp, he took the oath of office. His father, who was a notary public, administered the oath. The only other witnesses were his wife, Grace; a stenographer; a chauffeur; a congressman; and two reporters, who were not allowed to take pictures. At 2:47 A.M. Coolidge signed the oath of office, making him the nation's 30th president.

The nation's 30th president was the quiet, reserved Calvin Coolidge. *(Library of Congress)*

"The man who builds a factory builds a temple."

—President Calvin Coolidge

Labor leader Samuel Gompers was president of the American Federation of Labor from 1886 until (with the exception of one year) his death in 1924. *(Library of Congress)*

Coolidge's health was not particularly robust. He may hold the distinction of being the sleepiest U.S. president—he usually slept about 12 hours a day.

BACKGROUND ON COOLIDGE

John Calvin Coolidge was born in Plymouth Notch on July 4, 1872. His father was a farmer and ran the local general store; his mother was the daughter of a prosperous local farmer. As a child, Calvin milked cows, split firewood, and helped his grandfather sharpen the scythes used to harvest the crops. He attended school in a one-room schoolhouse in Plymouth.

Coolidge graduated with honors from Amherst College in Massachusetts in 1895. The carefulness with money he would bring to the presidency was already apparent. During his college years, he kept precise accounts of the money he spent, and never once did he overspend his allowance. Also apparent early on was his modesty. During his senior year, he won a large cash prize in a college essay contest. He never mentioned this fact when he sought a job at the law firm in Northampton, Massachusetts, that hired him as a clerk.

Coolidge studied law for two years until he was admitted to the state bar in 1897. But his real love was politics. For the next two decades he climbed the political ladder as a conservative Republican in Massachusetts. He was a Northampton city councillor (1899–1902), state legislator (1907–09), mayor of Northampton (1910–11), state senator (1912–15), lieutenant governor (1916–18), and governor (1919–21). In the meantime, he married Grace Goodhue, a teacher of the deaf, in 1905.

Coolidge might never have entered national politics had it not been for a police strike in Boston in 1919. This strike, backed by the American Federation of Labor (AFL) union, was one of a wave of strikes that swept the nation in the years after World War I. Without police protection, Boston was in chaos. At first, Governor Coolidge did nothing, saying that he did not have the power to end the strike. But after two days of crime and looting, he called out the National Guard and the strike was put down. He made his intentions known to

AFL president Samuel Gompers in a one-sentence telegram: "There is no right to strike against the public safety by anybody, anywhere, any time."

When the contents of the telegram became public, Republican Party leaders concluded that Coolidge had the mettle they were looking for in a national leader. The result was that in 1920 he joined Warren Harding on the ticket as the surprise nominee for vice president, and the two handily defeated their opponents.

Just as Harding formed a sharp contrast with Woodrow Wilson before him, Coolidge was very different from Harding. Harding looked and sounded presidential; Coolidge was slight of build and reedy of voice. While Harding had extramarital affairs with several women and fathered an out-of-wedlock child, Coolidge was deeply attached to his wife and family. Harding's speaking style was often overblown and pompous; Coolidge was known as Silent Cal, the man who needed just one straightforward sentence to tell Gompers what he thought. While Harding liked to drink, play poker and golf, and while away time with friends, Coolidge was quiet, reserved, and cautious. He did, however, enjoy having his picture taken in Native American headdresses and cowboy outfits, while milking cows, or on his electrically operated artificial horse, which he rode three times a day. His Secret Service guards were frequent victims of his practical jokes.

"Battlin' Bob" La Follette of Wisconsin was an outspoken Progressive politician and candidate for president in 1924. *(Library of Congress)*

A DEADLY BLISTER

Life was still extremely precarious in the 1920s. In 1924, the president's younger son, Calvin Jr., died. He had played tennis in sneakers without wearing socks, causing a blister. The blister became infected, and the infection spread to his bloodstream, causing his death.

Antibiotics, such as penicillin, which can prevent or cure infections by killing microorganisms, had not been developed. Alexander Fleming discovered the ability of mold to kill bacteria in 1928, but the development of penicillin from that mold took a few more years.

Calvin Coolidge is depicted with his two sons, John and Calvin. Calvin died in 1924 of a blood infection. *(Library of Congress)*

Symbolic of the technological advances of the 1920s was radio equipment on a car used by Calvin Coolidge during his 1924 campaign. *(Library of Congress)*

First Lady Grace Coolidge, born Grace Goodhue, was a teacher of the deaf when she married Calvin Coolidge. *(Library of Congress)*

As vice president, Coolidge accomplished little. As president, though, he soon proved to be a capable administrator. During the early months of his presidency, he had to distance himself from the emerging scandals of the Harding administration to win the Republican Party's nomination for the 1924 presidential election. That year the Democratic Party, after 103 ballots, nominated John W. Davis, a corporate lawyer. Also running that year, on the Progressive Party ticket, was Wisconsin's Robert M. La Follette. La Follette was nationally known as Battlin' Bob for his vocal stands on such progressive issues as child labor and conservation. He also made the first U.S. political speech ever recorded on film with sound. Coolidge, with vice presidential candidate Charles G. Dawes of Illinois, won easily, tallying 15.7 million votes to 8.3 million for Davis and 4.8 million for La Follette.

THE FIRST LADY SPEAKS

Grace Coolidge found ways to let her views be known at a time when the first lady was supposed to retire into the background. She was an opponent of the Prohibition amendment but honored it by not serving alcohol at the White House. She lodged a protest, though, by naming her white collie Rob Roy, the name of a popular cocktail. (The president, in contrast, had a white collie named Prudence Prim.) One time, at a White House garden party, she had been instructed not to speak to the press. A reporter asked her a question she wanted to answer, so—having been a teacher of the deaf—she responded in sign language.

Laissez-faire is a French expression meaning roughly "to allow to do." It can refer to any system allowed to operate by itself without interference from authority.

THE LAISSEZ-FAIRE ECONOMY

Economic Growth

When Coolidge took office, the nation was still at peace, and Americans had made it clear that they wanted to remain withdrawn as much as possible from international affairs. For this reason, the focus of Coolidge's administration was the national economy. At the time of Harding's death, the nation was pulling out of the economic doldrums of the early 1920s. By reelecting Coolidge, Americans confirmed that they favored Harding's economic policies. It was during Coolidge's years in the White House that the 1920s really became the Roaring Twenties.

Coolidge continued most of the policies of his predecessor. In fact, the policies of the two presidents were so similar that many historians discuss the Harding-Coolidge years almost as one administration. Like Harding, Coolidge favored a balanced federal budget, lower federal spending, lower taxes, and high tariffs on foreign-made goods. Most important, he created a probusiness climate by adopting a laissez-faire

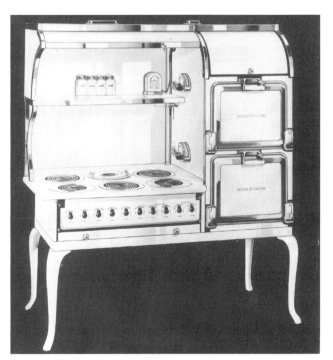

The electric oven/range, this one produced by General Electric, was one of many new or improved labor-saving devices that raised the standard of living for many Americans during the 1920s. *(Private Collection)*

Calvin Coolidge was devoted to his wife, Grace, although he could be a difficult husband. *(Library of Congress)*

BECK'S BIG WIN

The mood of political conservatism that had taken over the country was apparent virtually everywhere. In the mid-1920s, an extremely conservative politician named James Beck was elected to Congress. Beck ran in the poorest district of Philadelphia, a slum that was taking no part in the decade's prosperity. Still, he won his election with almost 97 percent of the votes cast.

philosophy—the principle that as much as possible the government should leave business alone and rely on the marketplace to create prosperity. Business leaders, of course, strongly supported the president. Perhaps the most famous statement Coolidge ever made reflected his probusiness stance: "The business of the United States is business."

This philosophy had both advantages and disadvantages. On one hand, the nation under Coolidge experienced rapid economic growth. The gross national product—the total value of all goods and services produced in the country—rose from $86.1 billion in 1923 to $98.2 billion in 1928, the last full year of Coolidge's presidency. Over the same time period, the total income of corporations rose from $119 billion to $153 billion. Americans were lured by effective advertising, frequent model changes, and easy credit into buying the many new and improved products that companies were turning out in ever greater volumes: radios, cars, vacuum cleaners, refrigerators, telephones, sewing machines…the list could go on and on. One reason Americans were able to do so is that they were working; in 1926, the unemployment rate was a mere 1.9 percent. It has been estimated that as much as 40 percent of the world's wealth was in U.S. hands at this time. Clearly, the United States was the most prosperous nation on earth. Little wonder that no one wanted to tamper with the mighty U.S. economic engine.

Americans wanted to share in the prosperity by buying shares of stock in corporations. This led to an enormous boom in the stock market. In 1921, the total number of stock shares that changed hands was about 173 million. That number increased steadily throughout the decade, rising to 1.1 billion shares in 1929. Americans watched the ticker tape, which sent information about transactions on the stock market, with as much interest as they followed the exploits of their favorite sports stars. The total value of these shares—on paper—quadrupled during the decade, as a growing number of buyers bid the prices up. This created a bubble of inflated stock prices that eventually had to burst. When it finally did, many investors were wiped out. But in the meantime, a stock market craze afflicted the nation.

Today's American Stock Exchange began as an outdoor "curb market" in the 1790s; it moved indoors in New York City's financial district in 1921. *(Library of Congress)*

The inflated stock market was only one of the problems the Coolidge administration failed to address. There were others that would overwhelm the economy after Coolidge left office.

Federal agencies such as the Federal Trade Commission had been created to regulate business. But they failed in their role as watchdogs because the people who ran them had close ties to business. The result was that many companies got away with fraud or misleading investors and the public.

The depression in farming continued, and industries such as coal mining and textile manufacturing were not doing much better. While the gross national product was going up, prices for the products of these industries were falling.

While mass production was bringing more goods to Americans than ever before, it became too easy to buy these goods on credit. Americans piled up a high volume of debt.

Income was distributed unevenly: By 1929, the 27,000 U.S. families with the highest incomes earned as much as the 11 *million* families with the lowest incomes.

Today, with the aid of computer technology, a billion shares would be an average day on Wall Street. In 1929, when all transactions were recorded on paper and processed by an army of clerks, a billion shares in a year was an astounding number.

Many American workers, such as those in the steel industry, demanded higher wages and often went out on strike in the early 1920s. *(Library of Congress)*

These and other problems eventually contributed to the severe economic depression of the 1930s. The Coolidge administration, though, seemed blind to them. In 1928, Coolidge told Congress, "The country can regard the present with satisfaction, and anticipate the future with optimism."

LABOR RELATIONS IN THE 1920S

Organized labor was still struggling for recognition in the 1920s. During World War I, labor had won some wage gains because of labor shortages and high production demands. But in the years immediately after the war, shortages of goods caused price increases, so labor found that it was falling behind again. Their wages remained low as prices rose.

The result was a wave of strikes between 1919 and 1922. In 1919, a full fifth, or 20 percent, of the U.S. labor force was on strike sometime during the year. In New England, garment workers, textile workers, and telephone operators went out on strike in 1919. That year, too, a general strike in Seattle paralyzed the city, and Massachusetts governor Coolidge had to put down the police strike in Boston. Late in the year, 400,000 coal miners and 300,000 steel workers went out on strike. On May 20, 1920, a dozen coal miners were shot and killed in Matewan, West Virginia, in a gun battle between miners (aided by the local sheriff) and mining-company thugs who were trying to stop striking miners from unionizing. In 1922, a massive machinists strike threatened to paralyze manufacturing industries.

This wave of strikes largely ended in 1922. After that, organized labor could boast of few gains for its members, and union organizers did not get much sympathy from

American businesses spent $1.8 billion on advertising during 1929.

the American public. Many Americans associated union activism with anarchy, socialism, and communism. They believed that foreign agitators, bent on overthrowing the U.S. government, were behind many of the strikes. Also, Harding and Coolidge enacted policies that were favorable to business. Business owners and operators, of course, always want to keep wages as low as possible, so wages rose only slightly during the 1920s. In 1924, the first full year of Coolidge's presidency, the average hourly earnings of a manufacturing worker were 54.7 cents an hour, or $23.93 per week. Wages remained about the same for the next several years. In 1928, the last full year of the Coolidge administration, they had risen to just 56.2 cents an hour, or $24.97 per week.

One reason that labor made such paltry gains in the 1920s was that the U.S. Supreme Court issued rulings that hurt labor unions. Among the most important cases was one called *Coronado Coal Co.* v. *United Mine Workers of America*. Although the events that gave rise to the case happened in 1914, the Supreme Court did not decide the case until 1925. The Court's decision reflected the probusiness climate of the 1920s.

In 1914, union coal miners working for the Coronado Coal Company in Arkansas went out on strike. The union's chief grievance was that the company was trying to use nonunion workers, who would work for lower wages. The strike turned violent: Striking workers destroyed company property at the mine, and two mining company employees were killed.

In suing the union for damages, the company used a ploy that business had been abusing for years: It said that the strike was illegal because it violated the Sherman Antitrust Act of 1890. This law made illegal any "contract, combination,…or conspiracy, in restraint of trade or commerce among the several States." The original purpose of the law was to restrain powerful business monopolies (large companies that control the market and drive out competition), but business owners

In 1900, Andrew Carnegie's income was $10 million. The average American's yearly income that year was $500.

In response to world criticism of American intervention in Nicaragua, President Coolidge said, "We are not making war on Nicaragua any more than a policeman on the street is making war on passersby."

turned it into a tool against organized labor. In *Coronado*, the company argued that the strike was illegal because it restrained trade. The Supreme Court agreed and ruled against the union.

The Court's decision in *Coronado* cast doubt on whether almost any strike was legal. All a company had to do now to fight union demands was to show that a strike restrained interstate trade, or trade across state borders. But the purpose of nearly any strike is to restrain trade, and the products of any large business are likely sold in more than one state. So the effect of the *Coronado* ruling was to say that any union strike could be considered a "combination in restraint of trade" and thus violated the Sherman Antitrust Act. Largely because of this and other Court rulings, union membership began to decline, and the number of labor strikes in the late 1920s remained low.

INTERNATIONAL RELATIONS

Neither Harding nor Coolidge placed much emphasis on international affairs. After World War I, Americans were weary of foreign entanglements, and Congress had reject-

U.S. Marines were sent to Nicaragua to stem revolution and the spread of communism in Central America. *(Library of Congress)*

SPYING IN THE 1920S

Today, it is taken for granted that the United States spies on other nations, especially its adversaries. In the 1920s, though, the United States did not do much spying. During World War I, the U.S. Navy had succeeded in deciphering coded German messages, but that effort ceased when the war ended. From 1919 to 1923, the U.S. Cipher Bureau was part of the War Department, but the bureau was quite small, consisting of only about a dozen codebreakers. After 1923, most intelligence on foreign countries was again gathered by the navy. By 1930, the navy was convinced that war with Japan was inevitable and stepped up its intelligence gathering in the Pacific.

Overall, U.S. authorities were reluctant to spy on other nations. In 1929, Secretary of State Stimson closed down the U.S. State Department's only cryptanalysis (codebreaking) organization, known as the Black Chamber. This agency had provided invaluable service over the previous 10 years and deciphered thousands of messages from dozens of nations. Stimson's remark about his distaste for spying remains famous: "Gentlemen do not read each other's mail."

Herbert Hoover's secretary of state, Henry Stimson, remains famous for expressing his distaste for espionage. *(Library of Congress)*

ed Woodrow Wilson's effort to join the League of Nations. But three international matters were noteworthy during Coolidge's term in office: American involvement in Central America, deteriorating relations with Japan, and the signing of the Kellogg-Briand Pact.

Central America

President Coolidge took steps to protect American business interests, including oil and sugar, in Central America, particularly in Nicaragua. President Harding had brought U.S. Marines home after 13 years of peacekeeping in Nicaragua; then, just 25 days later, a military uprising took place, so Coolidge turned the troops around and sent them back. He believed that Mexican revolutionaries were trying to export communism to Nicaragua, and that if the communists took over, they would seize U.S. businesses located there.

To resolve the situation, the president sent a New York trial lawyer, Henry Stimson, to the banks of the Tipitapa River in Nicaragua. There Stimson met in

During the 1920s, Japan began to flex its muscles in the Pacific; its growing industrial capacity is suggested by this photo of a Mitsubishi factory in Kobe, Japan. *(Library of Congress)*

In 1929 Kellogg was awarded the Nobel Peace Prize for his role in the Kellogg-Briand Pact.

the jungle with a rebel general named José María Moncada. Stimson, backed by 500 U.S. Marines, tried to persuade Moncada, backed by an army of rebels equipped with antique guns and knives, to surrender his army. Moncada agreed to make peace with the U.S.-backed government, but some of his generals refused to go along, leading to continued violence. What is important about this incident is that it began a long period, continuing into the 1980s, of U.S. intervention in Central America to resist the spread of communism.

Relations with Japan

In 1924, Japan was still rankled by its belief that the United States and the European powers had ignored it in the Treaty of Versailles after World War I. Then the United States passed the National Origins Act, which

Japanese officials called "the culminating act of rejection by the United States" because it seemed to identify the Japanese as a lesser race. The act further soured relations between the United States and Japan.

During the 1920s, Japan was beginning to flex its muscles in the Pacific. It launched an effort to dominate its area of the world. As an island nation, Japan depended on resources from other countries, and it tried to ensure reliable supplies of these resources—food, rubber, oil, and the like—by expanding its empire in the Pacific. In particular, it was building up its navy. It believed that the West, especially the United States but European powers as well, was trying to box it in and contain its growing power and influence. The United States tried to curb Japanese naval power at the Washington Conference in 1921 and 1922. The treaty the United States, Japan, and other countries signed, though, was violated as both the United States and Japan increased the size of their navies. Resentments that led to the 1941 Japanese attack on Pearl Harbor and the internment (confinement) of West Coast Japanese Americans during World War II began to fester during the 1920s.

The Kellogg-Briand Pact

The shadow of World War I and its horrors extended throughout the 1920s. Much of that war had been fought on French soil, so French foreign minister Aristide Briand proposed a treaty between France and the United States renouncing war as a means of settling disputes. Coolidge's secretary of state, Frank Kellogg, and others feared that signing such a pact would draw the United States into another European war if France were attacked. But not signing would make it appear that the United States was opposed to peace treaties. Kellogg took Briand's suggestion one step further and proposed that the treaty involve other nations. Briand agreed, and on August 27, 1928, the United States, France, Britain,

Secretary of State Frank Kellogg's name became part of the Kellogg-Briand Pact, a well-intentioned but meaningless international treaty outlawing war "as an instrument of national policy." *(Library of Congress)*

Grace Coolidge was an ardent baseball fan. She collected the scorecards of her favorite team, the Boston Red Sox, and was even invited to sit in the dugout with the team during the 1925 World Series.

SILENT CAL

One version of a story that is often told about Silent Cal goes as follows: At a state dinner, a woman seated next to him turned to him and said, "I made a bet with a friend that I could get you to speak three words to me tonight." Coolidge responded with two: "You lose." Coolidge was able to poke fun at his own reserve. Commenting on his wife, who was sociable and outgoing, he once quipped: "Having taught the deaf to hear, Miss Goodhue might perhaps cause the mute to speak."

Japan, Italy, Belgium, Poland, Czechoslovakia, and several other nations signed the Kellogg-Briand Pact, outlawing war "as an instrument of national policy."

The pact appealed to Americans who did not want the United States to go to war again. Its signing was met with great celebration; perhaps World War I really had been the "war to end all wars." But the pact was an utter failure. Diplomats did not take it seriously because they knew it could not prevent war. On the day that the U.S. Senate ratified the treaty, January 16, 1929, its next order of business was to appropriate $274 million to build warships. Just 14 years later, all the nations that signed the pact were at war.

In 1928 Coolidge decided not to run for a second full term. "When a man begins to feel that he is the only one who can lead in this republic," Coolidge once said, "he is guilty of treason to the spirit of institutions." He returned to Massachusetts, where he wrote his autobiography and a newspaper column entitled "Thinking Things Over with Calvin Coolidge." He died in Northampton on January 5, 1933.

CHAPTER 5

THE COOLIDGE YEARS: HARDING'S LEGACY, 1924–1925

P RESIDENT CALVIN COOLIDGE IN-
herited from Warren Harding more than an
improving economy. The first part of Coolidge's
presidency was marked by a number of key events that
reflected important social trends of the era. Prohibition
continued to be a divisive issue, and in this climate the
infamous gangster Al Capone made his first public
appearance. Anti-immigrant sentiment achieved legal
backing with National Origins Act of 1924, while the

President Calvin Coolidge, who
assumed the presidency on the
death of Warren Harding, is
driven to his first formal
inauguration accompanied
by Senator Charles Curtis.
(Library of Congress)

The public's fascination with Al Capone continues into the 21st century. Near the town of Couderay, in northwest Wisconsin, tourists can visit Capone's backwoods hideout, complete with a gangster museum, guided tours, souvenir shops, fine dining, and a snack bar that sells, of course, Chicago-style hot dogs.

Sacco-Vanzetti trial polarized national opinion. The ongoing conflict between progressive big-city life and rural religious fundamentalism was played out on the national stage in the so-called Scopes Monkey Trial of 1925. Popular entertainment trends began to sweep the nation as never before, helped by the rapidly expanding technologies of radio and movies with sound.

RISE OF AL CAPONE AND GANGSTERISM

One of the most enduring images of the Roaring Twenties is of its big-city gangsters—as well as such dedicated federal agents as Eliot Ness and his Untouchables, who fought them and could not be bribed. Synonymous with 1920s gangsterism is the name Al Capone (1899–1947), whose picture first appeared in Chicago newspapers in 1924 after he murdered a rival gangster named Joe Howard. (Capone was never charged because witnesses to the crime either disappeared or could not remember what they had seen.) Capone virtually ruled Chicago in the 1920s.

Alphonse "Scarface" Capone inherited his empire from the so-called father of American gangsterism, John Torrio. Torrio had put the Chicago mob together and used violence and bribery to turn a network of brothels (houses of prostitution) and gambling dens into a multimillion-dollar business. In 1919, he hired Capone, a hot-tempered bully, as his triggerman—the man who did the shooting when Torrio ordered. After the Prohibition amendment was passed, Torrio and Capone saw a new business opportunity. They promptly bribed the police and corrupt Chicago mayor "Big Bill" Thompson so that they could run speakeasies and bootleg liquor operations without police interference.

Torrio and his gang divided up the turf in Chicago with other mobsters. But Big Bill Thompson lost his reelection bid in 1923 to William Dever, who was honest and enforced the law. The bootleggers' profits began

BOISTEROUS BOOTLEGGERS

Al Capone was not the only bootlegger and gangster to win attention from the public. In New York City, the infamous Texas Guinan would sit on top of a piano in her speakeasies and greet her customers with "Hello, sucker!" She was hauled off in a paddy wagon in 1927, flashing a big smile at photographers and predicting that she would never spend a day in jail. She was right, for her business partner had influence with a corrupt city official.

Then there was George Remus, who is thought to be the model for Jay Gatsby, the title character of F. Scott Fitzgerald's classic novel about 1920s excess, *The Great Gatsby*. Remus was a bootlegger, but at least he was generous to his friends. One time he invited 200 guests to his estate, where he gave each male guest diamond cuff links and a pin, gifts whose total worth was $25,000, and each female guest, a hundred of them, a shiny new Ford automobile.

Remus amassed his fortune by bribing Jess Smith from the Department of Justice to get permits to buy liquor for medicinal purposes.

Al Capone was a notorious bootlegger and gangster who virtually ruled Chicago during the 1920s. *(Library of Congress)*

to fall, so rival gangs started invading one another's turf in an effort to make more money. The result was an outbreak of machine-gun violence between rival gangs, much of it at the hands of Capone, who took over Torrio's business when the elder man was shot. By 1929, Capone was behind at least 300 shooting deaths. The most infamous of these were the result of the St. Valentine's Day Massacre in 1929, when Capone's thugs murdered seven members of the rival Bugs Moran gang. Authorities were never able to make criminal charges stick.

Capone cut a colorful figure, and many Americans were captivated by him. He wore a $50,000 diamond ring. His seven-ton bulletproof limousine was actually a bit of a tourist sight in Chicago. He often conducted press conferences while wearing silk monogrammed pajamas. Throughout his infamous career, he portrayed himself as an innocent businessman who was simply trying to provide a service to his fellow man. Though he never was convicted of murder, he finally went to prison when he was convicted of tax evasion in 1931.

Eliot Ness became a well-known opponent of gangsters such as Capone. *(Corbis)*

Singer Ruth Etting performs the song "Big Bill the Builder" for Big Bill Thompson, the corrupt mayor of Chicago in the early 1920s. *(Library of Congress)*

Texas Guinan was a well-known New York City bootlegger. *(Library of Congress)*

IMMIGRATION

One of the most important issues that faced both the Harding and Coolidge administrations was immigration. In 1924, Congress passed the National Origins Act, which President Coolidge signed into law. This law was important because it severely restricted the number of immigrants that could be admitted to the United States. The law was the end result of several decades of prejudice against foreigners, especially foreigners from certain parts of the world.

Prejudice against Foreigners

In the 19th century, most immigrants to the United States had come from northern European countries. These countries included England, Ireland, Germany, and the Scandinavian countries, though many of immigrants on the West Coast were from China. But around 1890 the ethnic makeup of immigrants began to change. Slavs, Hungarians, southern Italians, Greeks, Romanians, and eastern European Jews came to the United States in growing numbers. Between 1892 and 1914, 17 million immigrants passed through Ellis Island, the New York City port where immigrants were admitted to the country. Most were from eastern and southern Europe. By 1910, immigrants and their children born in America made up 40 to 50 percent of the U.S. population.

It was not long before Americans from old immigrant groups—northern Europeans—began to argue that the hordes of immigrants from what they considered less desirable countries were bringing nothing but dirt, disease, and crime. To many, they were strange and exotic looking, and so, it was believed, they could not become part of the American melting pot. (Secretary of Labor James J. Davis called the new immigrants "rat people.") The Immigration Restriction League, which

Italian immigrants arrive at Ellis Island, in New York City harbor, in the 1920s. *(Library of Congress)*

ANTI-POLISH WORDS

Here is a typical comment about eastern European immigrants from the influential journal *Current Opinion*, April 1924.

There is no blinking the fact that certain races do not fuse with us, and have no intention of trying to become Americans. The Poles, for example, are determined to remain Polish. No doubt this is good Polish patriotism, but it is very poor Americanism. The Polish Diet [legislature], as the Indianapolis News points out, has adopted a resolution asking the government to request the Holy See

[the Vatican, seat of the Catholic Church] to use its influence with the Catholic hierarchy in the United States to permit the continued use of the Polish language in Polish Catholic churches and parochial schools. A dispatch from Warsaw declares that the resolution is part of an effort to stop "the systematic Americanization of the Poles"! Nevertheless, as the News declares, if we are to permit any Poles to come here in future, "the systematic Americanization" of them must continue.

A Crosley radio cost about $50—roughly two weeks' earnings for the average industrial worker.

"Many editorial observers warn us… that the United States has reached a 'point of saturation' where it cannot properly assimilate the foreign elements already here; and that failure to recognize this fact may result in the loss of the 'American type.'"

—*Literary Digest,*
December 18, 1920

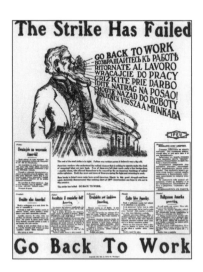

This strikebreaker poster reflected concern about widespread labor unrest during the early 1920s.
(Library of Congress)

believed in Nordic (northern European) genetic superiority, began to campaign for restrictions on immigration. Fueling their efforts was the outbreak of World War I, when foreigners were regarded as suspect. Defenders of immigration pointed out that these immigrants had provided much of the labor that turned the United States into an industrial power. It was this industrial might that enabled the United States to win World War I. After the war, these defenders faced an uphill battle. Many Americans were frightened by the large number of immigrants who were fleeing the poverty and starvation of post-world-war Europe. Organizations such as the Ku Klux Klan stoked this fear. As a result, by the early 1920s Americans were calling for immigration restrictions.

Red Scares

Also fueling prejudice against foreigners was the effect of the Russian Revolution of 1917. Many Americans came to see all Jewish people and those from the Slavic regions of eastern Europe as Bolsheviks, referring to the communist political party that had seized power after the Russian Revolution. Critics of immigration saw these immigrants as a threat to American security. A number of incidents seemed to strengthen their case. In 1919, many eastern European workers took part in a violent strike against the steel industry. This strike was a portion of a great deal of unrest that rocked the United States that year and into the early 1920s, including race riots in 25 American cities. Anarchists (those who do not believe in any form of government), socialists, and communists openly threatened to overthrow capitalism and the U.S. government.

Americans were especially frightened of communists. This fear led to what are called the Red scares, the suddenly widespread belief that communists and other foreigners were plotting a revolution in the United

States. This fear grew when a bomb exploded at the house of U.S. attorney general A. Mitchell Palmer in Washington, D.C., on June 3, 1919. The same night, seven other powerful bombs exploded in cities across the country. Still other bombs were mailed to financier J. Pierpont Morgan, industrialist John D. Rockefeller, Secretary of Labor William Wilson, and Supreme Court Justice Oliver Wendell Holmes Jr. In an odd twist of fate, these bombs were not delivered because they did not have enough postage.

The result was the so-called Palmer raids, which began in late 1919 and continued into 1920. During these raids, the police rounded up and arrested people who were thought to belong to radical political groups. Eventually, up to 10,000 people were arrested. Hundreds of those arrested were deported. Then on September 16, 1920, a bomb went off in the heart of New York City's financial district, at Wall and Broad Streets. As a result, 28 people were killed, and more than 200 were injured. Most Americans believed that foreigners were behind these outrages and called for immigration reform.

Fear of anarchy grew after an explosion rocked the home of U.S. attorney general A. Mitchell Palmer in 1919. *(Library of Congress)*

The Sacco-Vanzetti Case

One incident that dominated the headlines of American newspapers deepened this prejudice against foreigners. On April 15, 1920, a paymaster and a guard were shot dead during a holdup in Braintree, Massachusetts. The robbers made off with $16,000. Five men took part in the holdup, but only two were arrested, Nicola Sacco and Bartolomeo Vanzetti, three weeks after the crime. The names Sacco and Vanzetti are to this day linked to one of the most controversial legal cases of the 1920s.

Anarchist bombings, such as this one in New York City, created widespread fear that foreign subversives wanted to overthrow the U.S. government. *(Library of Congress)*

LETTER FROM NICOLA SACCO TO HIS SON

Just nine days before his death, Nicola Sacco sent a letter to his son Dante from the Charlestown State Prison. Publication of this letter greatly increased sympathy for him. Following are some excerpts from the letter, reprinted exactly as he wrote it, with all its mistakes.

Since the day I saw you last I had always the idea to write you this letter, but the length of my hunger strike and the thought I might not be able to explain myself, made me put it off all this time....

Much we have suffered during this long Calvary. We protest today as we protested yesterday. We protest always for our freedom.

If I stopped hunger strike the other day, it was because there was no more sign of life in me. Because I protested with my hunger strike yesterday as today, I protest for life and not for death.

But remember always, Dante, in the play of happiness, don't you use all for yourself only, but down yourself just one step, at your side and help the weak ones that cry for help, help the prosecuted and the victim, because that are your better friends; they are the comrades that fight and fall as your father and Bartolo fought and fell yesterday for the conquest of the joy of freedom for all and the poor workers. In this struggle of life you will find more love and you will be loved....

I feel better that you did not come to the death-house so that you could not see the horrible picture of three lying in agony waiting to be electrocuted, because I do not know what effect it would have on your young age. But then, in another way if you were not so sensitive it would be very useful to you tomorrow when you could use this horrible memory to hold up to the world the shame of the country in this cruel persecution and unjust death. Yes, Dante, they can crucify our bodies today as they are doing, but they cannot destroy our ideas, that will remain for the youth of the future to come.

Many Americans believed that the trial and conviction of Nicola Sacco and Bartolomeo Vanzetti for robbery and murder was unfair and reflected prejudice against southern European immigrants. *(Library of Congress)*

The two men, both Italian immigrants, were tried in an atmosphere of Red hysteria. They were found guilty on July 14, 1921, and both were executed on August 23, 1927. To this day, historians debate their guilt or innocence. Some point out that both men had called for the violent overthrow of the U.S. government. Both were associates of other anarchists, including those responsible for the bombs that exploded in Attorney General Palmer's house and on Wall Street. Further, the bullet that killed the paymaster came from a gun found on Sacco at the time of his arrest. Even if neither of the men pulled the trigger, they were very likely part of the plot. On the night of their arrest, they were caught concealing dynamite.

Other historians are not so sure of their guilt. They believe the men were the victims of prejudice against foreigners. They argue that the men were convicted because of their radical political beliefs, not because the evidence proved their guilt. They point out that witnesses confirmed Sacco's alibi: He said he was at the Italian consulate inquiring about a passport for his son on the day of the murders. At the time, some people called the verdict "judicial murder" and expressed great sympathy for Sacco and Vanzetti. The two became martyrs for political radicals in the 1920s and 1930s.

The question persists: Did Sacco and Vanzetti receive a fair trial? Either way, the case strengthened negative stereotypes about southern Europeans. It sharpened the debate between those who wanted to restrict immigration and those who wanted the United States to continue to be a haven for the world's poor and oppressed.

The National Origins Act of 1924

It was in this climate that the National Origins Act was made law in 1924. This law, though, was not the first law designed to restrict immigration. In 1920, California passed a law prohibiting new Japanese immigrants from owning land. In 1921, the Emergency Immigration Act had limited the number of immigrants allowed to 3 percent of the foreign born of each nationality already living in the country. This limitation ensured that immigrants from countries that had long been sending people to the United States, primarily northern European countries, would be favored.

The word *red* has always been associated with communism because of the red flags commonly used by revolutionaries in the 19th century.

THE MELTING POT

The Melting Pot was the title of a popular 1908 play written by Israel Zangwill. In a melting pot, metals are heated until they liquefy and mix, often becoming a stronger alloy than the original, separate ingredients. Zangwill did not invent the phrase, but his play helped popularize the term. The term *melting pot* refers to how immigrants from all over the world came to the United States, eventually lost their original habits and culture, and were mixed into a greater whole, or assimilated, as Americans.

OUT IN THE COLD

Russia had been largely ignored in the Treaty of Versailles, which some believe helped cause the treaty's failure. Russia had lost 1.7 million combatants and withdrew from the war in 1917. That year, a revolution in Russia ended the rule of the czars, or the Russian royalty, and enabled the Bolshevik Party under communist Vladimir Lenin to seize control. Many Americans and Europeans were suspicious of socialism and communism. Thus, despite its immense losses during the war, Russia was given little role in shaping the peace.

"The new selective law is just beginning to function. It is more pleasant now for the immigrants."

—Secretary of Labor James J. Davis reporting on a visit to Ellis Island, *New York Times,* July 20, 1924

In 1924, the Emergency Immigration Act was due to expire. Congress felt that a new law to replace it was urgently needed. The new law was sponsored by Representative Albert Johnson (1869–1957), who was a member of an organization called the Asiatic Exclusion League, and Senator David Reed (1880–1953). The National Origins Act is therefore sometimes referred to as the Johnson-Reed Act.

Johnson devised a formula that would cut the total number of immigrants allowed to 161,000, though that number was later lowered to 150,000. Each nation was assigned a quota—2 percent of its number already in the United States according to the 1890 census, greatly favoring old immigrant countries. (Eastern and southern Europeans arrived in large numbers only after 1890.) Reed, though, thought that using the 1890 census would appear to be too discriminatory toward new immigrant countries. He proposed using the 1920 census to establish the quotas, though he believed that using the later census would have nearly the same effect as using the 1890 census would have. His version of the bill won, and President Coolidge signed it into law.

The act immediately met with a storm of protest. Newspapers published by Italians, Poles, Jews, Armenians, and other ethnic groups were sharply

DIEGO RIVERA

Diego Rivera (1886–1957) was famous among the muralists, including Jose Clemente Orozco and David Siqueiros, who founded the school of Mexican painting. He ranks as one of the foremost painters of the 20th century. In 1920, he traveled to Italy where he studied the great frescos of the Italian Renaissance painters, who worked in the early 1500s. But his politics and social outlook were very modern. He supported Mexican resistance to foreign domination.

He was a member of the Communist Party in Mexico, and he briefly taught art in Moscow in the Soviet Union, which was ruled by the Communist Party. Reaction to the social and political themes of his work sometimes reflected the fear of communism at the time.

LIBERTY TRE

STAMP ACT

THE FOLLY OF ENGLAND THE RUIN OF AMERICA

critical. They thought that the act identified them as inferior races. The act had one other far-reaching effect. Between 1924 and 1929, 300,000 eastern European Jews were denied entry to the United States. Some of these people could have been saved from the Holocaust (the systematic slaughter of Jews in German Nazi-occupied Europe) during World War II had they been admitted. Nonetheless, the act provided the framework for American immigration policy until the 1960s.

Diego Rivera was the most famous Mexican muralist, though some Americans took exception to the socialist and communist themes in some of his work. *(Library of Congress)*

José Clemente Orozco was a well-known Mexican muralist in the American Southwest in the 1920s.
(Library of Congress)

Effect on Hispanics

A further effect of the National Origins Act, although an indirect one, was to sharply increase the number of Mexican immigrants to the United States. Because the act was directed primarily against eastern European and Asian immigrants, countries in the Western Hemisphere were exempt from the act. Thus, during the 1920s, as many as a half million Mexicans crossed the border to the United States. Many of these immigrants were illegal, but immigration enforcement at the border with Mexico was lax because these immigrants provided cheap labor in agriculture, mining, the railroads, and the steel and auto industries.

Until the end of World War I, Mexican and other Hispanic immigrants were concentrated primarily in the border states near Mexico: Texas, New Mexico, Arizona, and southern California. Most immigrants headed for company towns and agricultural work camps in these states. Since race issues nationwide focused on tensions between whites and African Americans, Hispanics were hardly noticed. This began to change during the 1920s. While many Mexican workers continued to look for jobs in agriculture and mining in the Southwest, many more were beginning to settle in urban areas in the north and Midwest, often looking for jobs that had formerly been taken by eastern European immigrants. As the decade progressed, these workers were not always welcomed, for the Great Migration of African-American workers from the South was helping to fill labor needs. Hispanic immigrants either settled in segregated barrios, were sent back to Mexico, or drifted back to the Southwest on their own.

One lasting cultural legacy of Mexican immigration from this era was an artistic movement called Mexican muralism. This movement provided the first major visual art form in the United States that did not originate in Europe. During the 1920s, such famous Mexican artists as Diego Rivera, José Clemente Orozco, and David

Alfaros Siqueiros created large murals on prominent public buildings throughout the Southwest. These murals depicted scenes from Mexico's history; many contained political and social messages. Visitors to such Arizona cities as Phoenix and Tucson can still see these colorful murals. They preserve the cultural ties of the Hispanic community in the Southwest from the 1920s.

THE SCOPES MONKEY TRIAL OF 1925

Perhaps no episode of the 1920s marked the tension between modern urban life and small-town life more than the Scopes Monkey Trial of 1925. The opponents in the trial were a high school teacher (John Scopes) from Dayton, Tennessee, and the state of Tennessee. But the real opponents during the trial were the forces of scientific thinking versus an older, religiously conservative fundamentalism. Small-town and rural Americans who believed in old-time religion felt more and more that their way of life was being threatened by modern, so-called godless scientific thinking, so they fought back.

One way they fought back was by opposing the teaching of evolution in schools. During the early 1920s, bills against the teaching of evolution were introduced in six states throughout the South. These bills would have made it against the law to teach that humans evolved from lower animals such as monkeys or apes and that the account of creation contained in the Bible was not literally true. By 1925, two such bills had been defeated, but three were still pending. The bill had passed in Tennessee, but no one really believed that the law would ever be enforced.

The American Civil Liberties Union (ACLU), an organization dedicated to defending the Constitution's Bill of Rights, believed the new law violated the right to free speech. It hoped that someone would be convicted of violating the law so that it could support an appeal of the ruling in a higher, federal court and get the law

The trial of John Scopes for teaching evolution in Tennessee was symbolic of the divide separating big-city sophistication and small-town conservatism during the 1920s. *(AP/Wide World)*

THE URBAN SHIFT

The tension between small town and city is reflected in the change in the relative populations of urban and rural areas by 1920. In 1910, most Americans—49.9 million—had still lived in rural communities with populations under 2,500, while 42 million lived in communities larger than 2,500. By 1920, the balance had shifted to 51.5 million (rural) versus 54.1 million (urban). This shift continued throughout the 1920s. By 1930, the numbers were 53.8 million (rural) versus 68.9 million (urban).

Clarence Darrow served as the defense attorney during the Scopes Monkey Trial in 1925. *(Library of Congress)*

"...of course like every other man of intelligence and education I do believe in Organic Evolution. It surprises me that at this late date such questions should be raised."

—Woodrow Wilson, August 29, 1922

struck down. So the ACLU took out an ad in the *Chattanooga News,* offering to finance the defense of anyone who challenged the law by teaching evolution. A group of town boosters in Dayton, perhaps wanting to put their small town on the map, came up with a plan. They persuaded John Scopes, a 24-year-old high school physics teacher, to test the law. Oddly, Scopes had never actually taught evolution; he filled in one day for the school's biology teacher and assigned textbook pages that discussed evolution. But he was charged with violating the law and brought to trial.

The Scopes Monkey Trial, as it came to be called, became a sensation. It was the first jury trial brought to the public live by radio. The atmosphere in Dayton during those hot July days became carnival-like. Hundreds of people came to town in horse-drawn wagons and Model T automobiles to see the trial. Evangelists set up tents. Vendors sold hot dogs and toy monkeys in the streets near the courthouse steps. One man brought two live chimpanzees "as witnesses for the prosecution," he said. More than 200 reporters from across the nation wired dispatches to their newspapers about the course of the trial. At one point, a group of them climbed onto a table in the back of the courtroom to get a better view. The table collapsed, dumping them onto the floor. The judge could barely restore order among the rowdy spectators.

One reason the public was so interested was that they knew the attorneys who argued the case. Leading the prosecution was William Jennings Bryan (1860–1925). Bryan, himself a product of rural America, had run for president three times, losing each time. Known as the Great Commoner, he was a hero to rural America and those who believed in traditional religion. Scopes's legal team called in big-city lawyer Clarence Darrow (1857–1938), who had earned a reputation as a brilliant defense attorney. Both men were gifted orators. Their struggle resembled a match between two world-champion heavyweight boxers.

During the trial, Darrow tried to introduce modern scientific evidence in support of evolution. The judge excluded such evidence, saying that the sole issue was whether or not Scopes had taught evolution. In a desperate but brilliant move, Darrow called Bryan himself to the stand—as a witness for the defense. Bryan agreed to testify as an expert on the Bible. In a dramatic exchange between the two that lasted throughout the day, Darrow humiliated Bryan by forcing him to admit that Jonah had been literally swallowed by a big fish, that the first woman's name was Eve and that she had been made from Adam's rib, and that a flood in 2348 B.C. had wiped out all living things except for those on Noah's ark. At one point, Bryan lost his temper; Darrow responded with equal heat. The spectators were about to riot when the judge adjourned court for the day. The next day, he ordered Bryan's testimony stricken from the record.

For many Americans, Clarence Darrow was a hero for his defense of progressive thinking. *(Private Collection)*

"The Christian parents of the state owe you a debt of gratitude for saving their children from the poisonous influence of an unproven hypothesis."

—William Jennings Bryan, telegram to Governor Austin Peay

The common nickname given to the Model T was Tin Lizzie. It developed about 20 horsepower and could reach a top speed of 45 miles per hour.

The Scopes Monkey Trial was immortalized in a Broadway play by Jerome Lawrence called *Inherit the Wind.* The play was turned into a Hollywood motion picture with the same title in 1960. The title is taken from the biblical book of Proverbs 11:29: "He that troubleth his own house shall inherit the wind."

THE BIRTH OF TV

Television technology also developed in the 1920s. On April 7, 1927, the first television broadcast took place. That day, future president Herbert Hoover gave a speech in Washington, D.C. He could be heard and seen (barely) on a tiny, primitive television screen in New York City. The Great Depression, then World War II, delayed the introduction of TV to the American home until the late 1940s.

The jury found Scopes guilty, and the judge fined him $100. This fine turned out to be the undoing of the ACLU, for the judge technically violated the law. The jury was supposed to have imposed the fine, not the judge. So when the case was appealed to the Tennessee Supreme Court, the court overturned the conviction because of the fine and sent the case back to the lower court. Scopes had technically won, but the higher court never resolved the free speech issue. Because the case was never retried, fundamentalists felt that they had won. Newly energized, over the next two years they backed antievolution bills in 12 states. The legislature in Mississippi passed such a bill, and a similar law was passed by popular referendum in Arkansas. (In a referendum, citizens, rather than their elected representatives, vote on whether to enact a law.) The issue of teaching evolution was not settled until 1968, when the U.S. Supreme Court ruled that the Arkansas law was unconstitutional.

Five days after the Scopes trial, Bryan, exhausted by the heat, collapsed and died. He remained a hero to defenders of older religious and small-town values. Darrow went on to a career as a writer and lecturer. Until his death he was a hero to intellectuals and those who backed more modern, scientific views.

LIFE IN THE 1920S

The 1920s was an era of magic. Americans marveled at the magic shows of such master illusionists and escape artists as Harry Houdini and Carter the Great, who toured from city to city and performed before thousands of awed spectators.

But the 1920s was also an era of another kind of magic—the magic created by scientists, inventors, engineers, technicians, businesses. Some of these developments were improvements in existing technology, such as the telephone and airplane. Others were new products that made life a little more fun: PEZ candy was developed in 1927, bubble gum in 1928. Still others were products that made life in the home a little easier: the Band-Aid in 1920, the aerosol can in 1927, the electric shaver in 1928, frozen food in 1929. Research scientists made discoveries that would later have far-reaching consequences: the liquid-fuel rocket was invented in 1926; penicillin (the first antibiotic used to fight infectious diseases) was discovered in 1929. It was an era when Americans began to think that anything was possible.

Among the technological advances of the 1920s, though, two stand out: radio and the automobile. Although both had been around since the 19th century, both spread rapidly in the 1920s, fundamentally transforming American life during those years and beyond.

Harry Houdini's name is still synonymous with amazing feats of magic and escape artistry. *(Library of Congress)*

Radio

The *mass media,* as the term is used today, had its roots in the 1920s. In virtually every city, numerous newspapers competed for the public's attention. Ethnic newspapers, appealing to immigrants from one country, were common in big cities. What today is called tabloid journalism—journalism that focuses on lurid or sensational stories—was commonplace in the 1920s.

The press, though, soon faced intense competition from a developing technology, radio. The first commercial radio station, WDKA in Pittsburgh, went on the air in 1920. In November of that year it aired the first broadcast of election returns for the Harding–Cox race. Few people, though, had radios, so an army of inventors and tinkerers went to work and developed affordable, but crude and unsightly, crystal sets. On a clear night, these crystal radios could pick up broadcasts from cities such as New York, Pittsburgh, and Philadelphia.

Then in 1922 the Crosley Radio Corporation came out with a line of radios, including do-it-yourself kits,

Harry Houdini, the most famous of the early 20th-century magicians, was born Eric Weisz in Hungary in 1874. His career reached its peak in the 1920s before his death in 1926.

The radio rapidly became a common article of furniture in the American home during the early 1920s. *(Library of Congress)*

Zane Grey (1872–1939), whose name is forever linked with popular images of the Old West, was by profession a dentist in New York City. He wrote nearly 80 books, and more than 100 movies have been made from his novels.

that relied on simpler vacuum tubes rather than crystals. The Crosley radios were the first with dials to adjust the volume and tune in to stations. Just as important, they were packaged in an attractive wooden case that looked more like furniture. So while in 1922 Americans had bought about $60 million worth of radio equipment, in 1923 that figure soared to $136 million and to $430 million in 1925. In 1922, 28 radio stations were in operation in the United States. By 1927, that number had risen to 681. The radio came to occupy the same position in the American home that the television would three decades later.

The radio rapidly became Americans' ear to the world. Before the 1920s, people received their news and information largely from the newspaper—if they could read, and if they had access to a newspaper. It could take days, even weeks, for information to filter out to small towns, rural areas, and even larger towns and cities in isolated parts of the country. The audiences for music, theater, and sports were limited to those who could get themselves to the event. The radio, though, turned the United States—from Los Angeles to New York and points in between—into a single stage. Suddenly, large numbers of people were receiving similar information, listening to the same music, and sharing a common mass culture, much like today. They could listen to Sunday sermons, talks on infant care and car repair, sports reports, boxing matches and baseball games, popular music (including jazz), comedy sketches, dramatic plays, and news. Advertisements created a demand for products that people might not have known even existed before. The radio also changed U.S. politics. Now candidates' voices could reach people whom the candidates themselves could never have reached in person. Calvin Coolidge was the first American president to have his inauguration (in 1925, when he was reelected) broadcast over the radio.

Radio could not have grown so rapidly without electricity, another modern miracle of technology that spread widely during the decade. In 1920, Americans consumed about 57 billion kilowatt-hours of electricity. By 1929, that number had risen to about 118 billion kilowatt-hours. In 1920, a third of U.S. homes had electricity; by 1929 the number of homes with electricity had doubled. Laborsaving electric appliances gave Americans more leisure time to gather around their new radio sets.

The Automobile

If it is impossible to overstate the effects of the radio on American life in the 1920s, it is also impossible to overstate the effects of the car.

In previous decades, isolated farmers, ranchers, and small-town folk could travel in a day only as far as a horse and wagon could carry them on a rutted, perhaps muddy, road. So they often just stayed home. With cars, now they could visit a nearby town more often to trade news, buy supplies, see a movie, or enjoy coffee or a sandwich with friends. City dwellers, too, had relied on horse-drawn carriages—or their feet—though they could board a train to travel longer distances. Now homemakers in towns and cities could run to the market whenever they wanted, changing patterns of food distribution and consumption.

New businesses grew up as roads made it easier to get places. Highway growth led to traffic lights (invented in 1923), billboard advertising, gas stations, motels, diners, roadside tourist attractions, traffic jams, and

Crystal radios use a germanium or lead sulfide diode to pick up the signal. Commercially made radios no longer use crystals, but many hobbyists continue to make them, often building them from simple parts and setting them in cylindrical oatmeal containers.

Henry Ford's company, which produced the Model T, dominated the automobile industry in the 1920s. *(Library of Congress)*

The 1920s witnessed the spread of automobiles, which were manufactured by dozens of companies until Ford, Chrysler, and General Motors came to dominate the industry. *(Private Collection)*

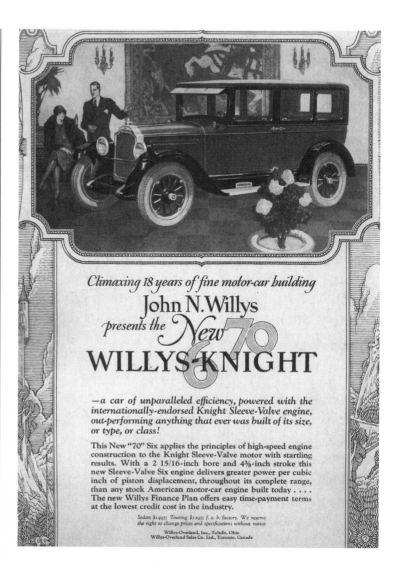

Climaxing 18 years of fine motor-car building
John N. Willys
presents the New 70
WILLYS-KNIGHT

—a car of unparalleled efficiency, powered with the internationally-endorsed Knight Sleeve-Valve engine, out-performing anything that ever was built of its size, or type, or class!

This New "70" Six applies the principles of high-speed engine construction to the Knight Sleeve-Valve motor with startling results. With a 2 15/16-inch bore and 4⅜-inch stroke this new Sleeve-Valve Six engine delivers greater power per cubic inch of piston displacement, throughout its complete range, than any stock American motor-car engine built today.... The new Willys Finance Plan offers easy time-payment terms at the lowest credit cost in the industry.

Sedan $1495; Touring $1295; f. o. b. factory. We reserve the right to change prices and specifications without notice

Willys-Overland, Inc., Toledo, Ohio
Willys-Overland Sales Co. Ltd., Toronto, Canada

"The old car was too slow.... The public was satisfied with it. And that's a sign we ought to change to something better. Now the public ought to have speed, since roads are so much better than they were. Therefore we gave it speed. That's the whole story of the new car."

—Henry Ford from the *New York Times Magazine,* January 8, 1928

other sights still familiar to American motorists. Around the edges of cities, green, leafy suburbs spread as commuters drove to the city to work. To the shock of some members of the older generation, dating and courtship moved from the parlor to cars parked in lovers' lanes, and young people could more easily escape the watchful eyes of their parents.

The numbers themselves tell the story of the automobile's astonishing growth during the 1920s.

In 1920, the number of registered cars was about 8 million. By the end of the Coolidge administration

in 1929, the number had grown to 23 million. In 1904, just 700 trucks were registered in the United States. In 1929 there were 3.4 million, carrying goods to new consumers. School buses made it possible for children to attend school farther away, so school districts began to merge.

In 1909, the United States had a total of 725 miles of paved rural roads. By 1930, 100,000 miles of rural roads were paved, linking cities and the country in new ways. The first filling station opened in 1913. In 1929, there were more than 121,000. In the decade after World War I, Americans spent $30 billion on cars. In 1924, drivers traveled 100 billion miles on the nation's highways.

In 1904, at the dawn of the automobile revolution, about 12,000 workers were involved in car production. In 1929, the number was 471,000. That figure does not include the thousands more who provided auto repairs,

The spread of the automobile changed patterns of dating and courtship among young Americans, often to the dismay of their elders. (*Library of Congress*)

The number of refrigerators manufactured rose from 5,000 a year in 1921 to a million in 1930.

While Ford was a brilliant engineer and businessman, he was otherwise ignorant and bigoted. He once said in public that the American Revolution of 1776 took place in 1812. He wrote anti-Semitic articles for newspapers and believed that a "Jewish conspiracy" was at work in the United States. His other most famous quote is "History is more or less bunk."

gas, and other services. And it does not include the increase in employment in the steel, petroleum, lead, plate-glass, leather, and other industries that provided parts for the auto industry. In 1929, the auto industry produced about 13 percent of the total value of U.S. manufactured products.

Henry Ford (1863–1947) was the industrialist who was responsible for much of this growth. Ford had founded the Ford Motor Company in 1903, determined to produce a car the common man could afford. He introduced the Model T in 1908, famously remarking that a customer could by a Model T in any color "so long as it is black." (Not until 1925 did the company offer a choice of colors.) In 1908, Ford made almost 11,000 cars, each selling for about $850. After he introduced assembly-line production in 1913, the company could make more cars and sell them at a lower price. Ford also began paying his workers $5 a day, a huge sum at the time, so they could afford the cars they were making. By 1916, the company was making more than 700,000 cars per year, each priced at $360. After World War I, the price continued to fall so that in 1924 one could be bought for $290. By 1925, Ford was making a car every 10 seconds. By the time production of the Model T ended in 1927, 15 million had been sold.

Throughout the first decades of the 20th century, scores of auto companies formed, then went out of business. But by the late 1920s, Ford was facing stiff competition from the nation's two other remaining automotive giants, General Motors and Chrysler. These companies, too, were producing lower-priced cars for average folk, but they were also producing higher-priced luxury models for the more affluent, cars that are valued collectors items today.

CHAPTER 6

THE COOLIDGE ADMINISTRATION: THE SECOND TERM, 1925–1928

THE ROARING TWENTIES REALLY CAME into their own during Coolidge's second term. He easily won the election in 1924 and officially began his elected term as president in March 1925. During the second half of the 1920s, Americans' fascination with technological progress was given a further boost by Charles Lindbergh's first-ever solo airplane flight across the Atlantic in 1927. During the second part of the Coolidge presidency, American Indians were finally granted full U.S. citizenship rights, and Americans began to recognize the poor conditions

The originator of the Charleston dance step, Frank Farnum, coaches actress Pauline Starke, who performed the dance in the film *A Little Bit of Broadway.* *(Library of Congress)*

"Billy" Mitchell, shown with an airplane, urged the government to upgrade the nation's air system. *(Library of Congress)*

American Indians were forced to endure. Jazz, sports, and movies flourished as never before. More and more, Americans took on the trappings of the 20th century.

THE LONE EAGLE: LINDBERGH'S FLIGHT

During the 1920s, aviation was still in its infancy. Planes had been used in World War I, but not nearly to the extent they are used in warfare today. The American public was not yet ready to accept commercial aviation. Trains were the primary means of transportation over long distances.

One person who tried to upgrade the nation's air system was Brigadier General William L. Mitchell (1879–1936). Mitchell had been a pilot during World War I. From 1920 to 1925, he was assistant chief of the army air service. He believed that airplanes would play a major role in warfare in the future and urged formation of a separate air force. His superiors, though, were not ready to listen. The top brass in the army felt threatened. They feared that an air force would make the army obsolete. But Mitchell pressed his point. In the summer of 1921 he staged an aerial bombing of a number of outdated U.S. ships and of German warships captured during World War I. His most spectacular success was in sinking one ship in 25 minutes using eight bombers.

Still, military authorities dragged their feet, and President Coolidge was reluctant to spend public money on warplanes. Frustrated, Mitchell publicly accused his superiors of incompetence. The result was that he was charged with insubordination, and his 1925 court-martial was highly publicized. Although he was found guilty, he attracted widespread public sympathy. People were beginning to believe that perhaps Mitchell was right—that air transportation had great potential, not

Charles Lindbergh was greeted with a ticker-tape parade when he returned to New York City after making the first nonstop solo flight across the Atlantic in 1927. *(Library of Congress)*

only for waging war but also for making travel easier and faster. The time was ripe for an event that would confirm this glimmering belief.

That event took place in 1927. On the morning of May 20, a small plane took off from an airstrip in Long Island, New York. In the cockpit was a young airmail pilot named Charles A. Lindbergh (1902–74), who had ordered and reconfigured a small monoplane (a plane with one set of wings instead of two or more) that he christened the *Spirit of St. Louis*. He arrived in Paris 33.5 hours later, where 100,000 people greeted him almost hysterically as a hero. Lindbergh had just completed the first solo nonstop flight across the Atlantic, earning the nickname the Lone Eagle.

Lindbergh's feat electrified the nation, indeed the world. The public's reaction to his flight foreshadowed the way Americans would greet astronauts returning

Boys were taught industrial skills, such as the operation of a laundry, at the Carlisle Indian School. *(Library of Congress)*

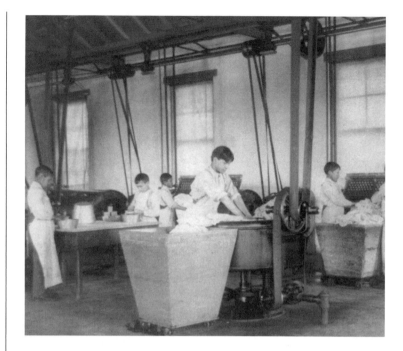

> *"…Not since the armistice of 1918 had Paris witnessed a downright demonstration of popular enthusiasm and excitement…."*
>
> —Edwin L. James, "Lindbergh Does It!…" *New York Times,* May 22, 1927

Jim Thorpe was later stripped of his Olympic medals when it was learned that he had been paid as a semiprofessional baseball player. In 1982, after numerous appeals, the International Olympic Committee finally returned his medals to the Thorpe family.

from space decades later. When he returned to New York, he was greeted by 200 boats and 75 planes. A ticker-tape parade showered him with 1,800 tons of paper. President Coolidge awarded him the Distinguished Flying Cross. Lindbergh became an overnight hero. A new dance, the Lindy Hop, was named for him, and the popular song "Lucky Lindy" celebrated his "peerless, fearless" feat. Lindbergh was young, daring, modest, clean cut, and handsome—an all-American boy. His flight convinced Americans that aviation would play an important role in their future.

AMERICAN INDIANS

Another American whose name was connected with heroic feats in the 1920s was known to most as Jim Thorpe (1888–1953). Thorpe was an athlete who had won two gold medals at the 1912 Olympic Games in Stockholm, Sweden. In the 1910s, he played six seasons with the New York Giants baseball team while at the same time playing professional football with the Bulldogs of Canton, Ohio. He was such a popular player that in 1920, when the National Football League was formed, he was appointed its first commissioner. He held this position while continuing to play professionally until 1928.

What made these accomplishments especially noteworthy for the 1920s was that his family knew Jim Thorpe by another name. For Thorpe had been born in Indian Territory, now Oklahoma, as Wa-tho-huck, an American Indian name meaning Bright Path. While Thorpe's path was indeed bright, the same could not be said about that of other American Indians during this era.

In the 1920s, American Indians were still suffering the ill effects of government policies from the 19th century. The 1887 General Allotment Act, also called the Dawes Act, had tried to assim-

ilate, or absorb, American Indians into European American culture by granting them 160-acre parcels of land they could work as farmers. The effect was to break up Native American communities and destroy traditional cultures and economic systems. Many American Indians lost their land to white settlers.

Additionally, the government set up a number of boarding schools for American Indians. Among the most famous of these was the Carlisle Indian School in Pennsylvania, whose most illustrious graduate was Jim Thorpe. The purpose of these schools was to train American Indians to become "Americans." The students were not allowed to play traditional games, speak

American Indian chiefs Frank Seelatse and Jimmy Noah Saluskin of the Yakima tribe posed for a portrait in front of the U.S. Capitol Building in Washington, D.C., in 1927. *(Library of Congress)*

SUPERSTAR PAY

In 1915, Thorpe was paid $250 per football game. At the time, such a sum was considered outrageously high. In contrast, Chicago Bulls basketball star Michael Jordan made more than $10,000 per minute of playing time at the height of his career in the 1990s. He earned $250 in about one and a half seconds on the court.

their native languages, or practice traditional religious beliefs. They wore uniforms, lived in military-style dormitories, and learned trades or, in the case of girls, domestic skills. Richard Henry Pratt, founder of the Carlisle School, summed up the philosophy: "Kill the Indian, save the man." In the meantime, the students' parents lived largely on reservations where poverty was the norm.

The 1920s, though, represented a turning point in relations between Native American tribes and the U.S. government. In 1921, the Snyder Act provided health care sponsored by the government to American Indians, and health conditions improved markedly; the number of cases of tuberculosis, for example, began to drop steadily. In 1924, during the Coolidge administration, American Indians were granted full U.S. citizenship rights under the Indian Citizenship Act. In the years that followed, a number of Native American chiefs were welcome guests at the White House and had their pictures taken with President Coolidge.

Then in 1926 a federal commission was formed to study life on the reservations and in the boarding schools. The result of this study was the 1928 Meriam Report, conducted by University of Chicago professor Lewis Meriam for the Department of the Interior. The Meriam Report pronounced the policies of the preceding 50 years a failure. It documented the poverty and malnutrition that prevailed on the reservations and the terrible effects of the boarding schools. It pointed out that the schools were a failure because of their destructive effects on Native American culture and the self-esteem of the students. In response to the report, a groundswell of support rose for a new policy toward American Indians, one that would foster traditional communities and customs. Congress responded in 1934 with the Indian Reorganization Act, which granted tribes the right to create formal governments and to manage their own reservations.

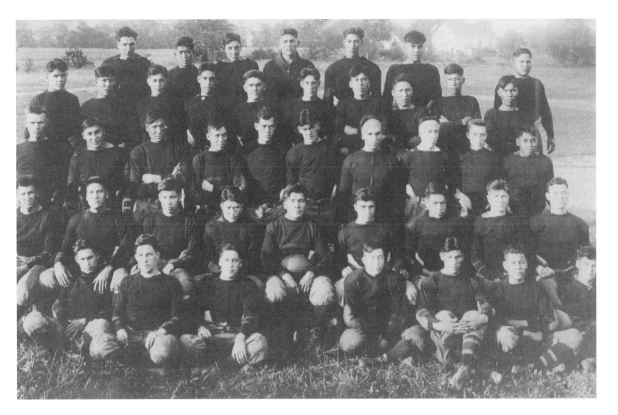

ROARING TWENTIES STYLE

After the horrors of World War I, many Americans in the 1920s sought pleasure and thrills. As author F. Scott Fitzgerald wrote, "The parties were bigger…the pace was faster…the shows were broader, the buildings were higher, the morals were looser and the liquor was cheaper." The car made Americans more mobile, so they could find amusement in new places. Rising standards of living gave them the money to pay for it. Developments in technology, including not just the car but also washing machines, fans, irons, electric stoves, refrigerators, vacuum cleaners, and the telephone, gave them more leisure time to seek out fads, fashions, and fun. Technology also made possible a new form of entertainment: movies.

A handful of developments stand out because they still affect popular culture today: jazz, movies, and sports.

As part of its effort to "Americanize" its students, the Carlisle Indian School in Pennsylvania maintained a highly successful football team. *(Library of Congress)*

Syncopation is a musical technique that shifts the accent to what is normally a weak beat. It gives music a funky, lilting rhythm.

Louis "Satchmo" Armstrong was one of the nation's most popular jazz musicians in the Roaring Twenties. *(RCA Corp.)*

Duke Ellington gave jazz a boost when he moved his act to the famed Cotton Club in Harlem, New York City, in 1927. *(Private Collection)*

Jazz

A defining feature of 1920s popular culture was jazz—so much so that the Roaring Twenties is also often called the Jazz Age. Jazz is a form of popular music that emphasizes a pulsing beat, syncopated rhythms, and improvisation (creating music on the spot without a fixed score). Its roots can be found in early types of African-American music, including ragtime, blues, and the African-American spiritual. While it originated in New Orleans, Louisiana, around the turn of the 20th century, it quickly spread to other parts of the country. Early musicians boarded riverboats traveling up the Mississippi River to take jazz to such cities as St. Louis, Memphis, Louisville, and Chicago. Among the most famous were Joe "King" Oliver and his Creole Jazz Band and trumpeter Louis "Satchmo" Armstrong. Early recordings of their music were at first marketed mostly to black audiences. Bix Beiderbecke, a white jazz trumpeter, helped make jazz more acceptable to white audiences, and soon jazz recordings were being purchased by audiences black and white. By the end of the 1920s, Americans in nearly every part of the country could listen to jazz either on the radio or in clubs. Jazz was modern—it was "hip to the jive"—and became the music of fun-seeking, up-to-date young people in much the same way that rock and roll would three decades later.

A key moment in jazz history took place in 1927. That year Edward "Duke" Ellington (1899–1974), the most famous jazz musician of them all, moved to New York City to perform at Harlem's Cotton Club, where his music was heard by the most sophisticated jazz listeners. He was a major innovator, and many of his compositions, including "Take the A Train" and "East St. Louis Toodle-oo," remain classics. In light of Ellington's huge success, other jazz bands formed, including those led by Fletcher Henderson, Cab Calloway, and Count Basie. These all-black bands were the forerunners of predominantly white swing orchestras in the 1930s, including those led by Glenn Miller and Jimmy Dorsey. They also influenced such mainstream 1920s composers as George Gershwin. Gershwin used jazz techniques in works that are standards today, including "Rhapsody in Blue" (1924) and "An American in Paris" (1928).

Movies: From Silent Screen to Talkies

By 1919, the infant film industry had moved from the East Coast to Hollywood, California. There, in the days before car exhaust and pollution had produced smog,

"I came away from the theater believing the days of sound were numbered."

—Charles Chaplin, recalling his first encounter with movie sound

Moviegoers were often awed by the elaborate scenes in films shot during the 1920s. *(Library of Congress)*

Actress Clara Bow gained fame as the "It" girl for her sex appeal, but she was never able to make the transition to "talkies," or movies with sound. *(Private Collection)*

The word *jazz* was first used in about 1913. Like many words for popular culture trends that defied traditional norms, jazz had a racy origin, referring initially to sexual relations.

the sky was almost always blue, and the weather rarely interfered with shooting. The films of the early 1920s were all silent films, though people did not watch them in silence. Even small movie houses usually hired a piano player to accompany the film, and the big movie palaces (some seating thousands of patrons) could afford to hire a small orchestra and create sound effects. During these years, the United States produced 80 percent of the world's motion pictures, in large part because the destruction of World War I in Europe set back the film industry there. Many European stars, including Sweden's Greta Garbo, were drawn to Hollywood, where an entire industry of agents, publicity directors, fan clubs, and celebrity gossip magazines was growing.

Throughout the 1920s, Americans went to the movies in growing numbers, drawn by their images of glamour, romance, and excitement—all presented in larger-than-life form on the big screen. Movies, unlike plays or vaudeville performances, were reproducible. They could be shown in hundreds of theaters at the same time, helping to create a mass culture that had never existed before. Hollywood satisfied the public's hunger for movies with such lavish spectacles as *The Ten Commandments* (1923) and *The King of Kings* (1927), both directed by the legendary Cecile B. DeMille. In 1926, the first film version of *Ben-Hur* was made for $4 million, an eye-popping figure for that time.

The film industry's biggest blockbusters were built on the popularity of some of its stars. Douglas Fairbanks was often cast as a swashbuckling hero in such costume adventures as *Robin Hood* and *The Three Musketeers*. Clara Bow, called the "It" Girl from her 1927 movie *It,* set the standard for sex appeal. Tom Mix was a major star as the tight-lipped hero in Westerns, while Charlie Chaplin and Buster Keaton raised comedy to a new level. But the most wildly popular film star of the era was Rudolph Valentino. Valentino, typecast as the smoldering Italian lover, was adored by millions of female fans for

RUDOLPH VALENTINO

Millions of American women wept openly on August 24, 1926, at the news that Rudolph Valentino, just 31 years of age, had died in New York City the day before. In response to the news, at least four women committed suicide.

Valentino's popularity was as great as that of any of today's sex symbols. As the Sheik, he caused American women to fantasize about being swept off their feet by an exotic, wealthy, handsome Italian lover and carried away to a rich world of guilty pleasure. His stardom is all the more astounding considering that in 1913 he stepped off a boat from Italy, could not speak English, and worked early on as a gardener.

Valentino's funeral was a circus. A huge mob of women came to the funeral home at Broadway and 66th Street in New York City. When the home did not open the doors, a near riot broke out. A large window was smashed, and many mourners were injured by flying glass. Mounted police could not control the crowd, so a hundred police reinforcements were called in. Finally the crowd broke up, but it returned the next morning. When the doors opened, women pushed and jostled each other to get a look at the Great Lover. By the end of the day, 50,000 women had passed before Valentino's open coffin.

Wildly popular actor Rudolph Valentino is depicted on the cover of *Motion Picture* magazine with his second wife, Natacha Rambova. Valentino married her in 1923, but when it was discovered that his divorce from his first wife was not official, he was jailed as a bigamist and fined $10,000. *(Private Collection)*

such 1921 movies as *The Four Horsemen of the Apocalypse* and, particularly, *The Sheik*. Equally adored, but by a different audience, was Mickey Mouse, who made his debut from the Disney studios in 1928.

For years, the film industry had been experimenting with ways to add sound to films. They failed because they could not amplify the sound enough, nor could they synchronize the sound on a phonograph record with the movie. Further, it would have been extremely expensive to add sound systems to existing movie theaters. In 1926, though, the Warner Brothers studio decided to take a risk and try a new sound technology called Vitaphone. The result was that on October 6, 1927, the company premiered the first sound film, *The Jazz Singer,* starring singer Al Jolson. The movie featured songs and some dialogue, but it was still partly silent. Then in 1928 Warner Brothers released *The Lights of New York*, the first all-talking motion picture. Soon other

MOVIE GOSSIP

Interest in the love lives of movie stars is by no means a modern development. Rumors of a love affair between John Gilbert and Greta Garbo, who costarred in a film in the mid-1920s, grabbed the attention of fan magazine and gossip column readers.

VOICELESS

The movie magazine *Photoplay* printed a short poem about the plight of an aspiring star whose voice was not suited to sound:

I cannot talk—I cannot sing
Nor screech nor moan nor
*   anything.*
Possessing all these fatal
*   strictures*
What chance have I in motion
*   pictures?*

Americans found thrills in magazines and newspapers, especially those that featured lurid and sensational stories. In 1919, the magazine *True Story* was founded, and by 1926 it had two million subscribers. They were drawn to stories with such titles as "The Primitive Lover," "Indolent Kisses," and "What I Told My Daughter the Night before Her Marriage." Also in 1919, the *New York Daily News* was founded. Just five years later, the newspaper, with screaming headlines over sex and crime stories, had the highest circulation of any daily newspaper in the country. *The Daily News* shocked even its own readers on January 13, 1928. Over the bold headline "Dead!" it printed a full-page picture of a woman named Ruth Snyder in the electric chair at the moment of her execution. Snyder had been convicted of murder in a sensational trial.

Even the stodgier *New York Times* could not resist a lurid story. Over a period of 20 days in 1926, it devoted 340,000 words to the scandalous trial of a New Jersey woman who had murdered her minister husband after discovering that he had a mistress. The trial featured courtroom readings of his candid love letters to the other woman.

Greta Garbo (1905–90) made 27 films in her career and, unlike many other performers, successfully survived the transition from silent films to the talkies. She was known not only for her acting talent but for her deep, sultry voice.

companies rushed to produce sound films. In 1928, only 1,300 of the 20,000 U.S. theaters were wired for sound. By the end of 1930, nearly 10,000 were wired.

The advent of the talkies had two major effects. One, it destroyed the vaudeville stage. Throughout the early and mid-1920s, silent films and vaudeville managed to coexist. After sound came to films, though, vaudeville could no longer compete and for the most part, it disappeared—in part because talented performers could make more money in a movie seen by millions than in a stage performance seen by just hundreds of people.

Two, the talkies also sunk the careers of many silent stars. The fate of actor John Gilbert, for example, was not unusual. Gilbert was a popular romantic actor, but the sound system, still not perfected, seemed to raise the pitch of his voice. Instead of sounding like a heartthrob, he sounded almost squeaky. At the same time the sound system made the voices of some popular actresses sound coarse and guttural. Further, because of the popularity of musicals, actors and actresses who could not sing were out of business. Even Clara Bow was unable to make the transition to talkies. Some performers, including Charlie Chaplin and actress Mary Pickford, believed that the talkies were a passing fad. They were, of course, wrong. In 1927, movie theater admissions totaled about 57 million per week. By 1930, that number had nearly doubled—about one movie per week for every man, woman, and child in the country. The talkies were here to stay.

Sports

The 1920s has often been called the golden age of sports in America. Many names from the decade's sports world remain legendary today. Red Grange, nicknamed the Galloping Ghost, electrified football fans of the University of Illinois and the Chicago Bears. Olympic

> **W**hen someone pointed out to Babe Ruth that his $80,000 salary was more than President Herbert Hoover's, he thought for a moment, then replied, "Well, I had a better year."

THE FORMATION OF THE NATIONAL FOOTBALL LEAGUE

Football was played professionally before the National Football League (NFL) was formed. No league existed, though, so teams did not always follow the same rules. So on August 20, 1920, an organizational meeting, attended by the Akron Pros, Canton Bulldogs, Cleveland Indians, and Dayton Triangles, was held at a Hupmobile (a brand of car) auto showroom in Canton, Ohio. The result was the formation of the American Professional Football Conference.

A second organizational meeting was held in Canton, Ohio, on September 17. The teams came from four states—Akron, Canton, Cleveland, and Dayton from Ohio; the Hammond Pros and Muncie Flyers from Indiana; the Rochester Jeffersons from New York; and the Rock Island Independents, Decatur Staleys, and Racine Cardinals from Illinois. The name of the league was changed to the American Professional Football Association. Four other teams— the Buffalo All-Americans, Chicago Tigers, Columbus Panhandles, and Detroit Heralds—joined the league during the year. The Decatur Staleys later moved to Chicago, where they became the Chicago Bears. On June 24, 1922, the league's name was changed to the National Football League.

Babe Ruth, possibly the most famous baseball player in history, electrified fans with his ability to hit home runs. *(Library of Congress)*

American boxing fans were thrilled when Jack Dempsey defended his heavyweight crown against French war hero Georges Carpentier in 1921. It was the first ever broadcast on radio and the first to produce gate receipts of a million dollars. *(Library of Congress)*

KID BLACKIE

In the 1910s, Dempsey went by the name Kid Blackie. He rode the trains from town to town, showed up at local gyms, and offered to take on all comers. In 1920, a jury acquitted him of draft evasion, and posters billed his 1922 fight against World War I pilot Carpentier as a battle of Good versus Evil.

swimmer Johnny Weissmuller went on to play the role of Tarzan in films; "Big Bill" Tilden and Helen Wills Moody ("Little Miss Poker Face") dominated men's and women's tennis. Among all the famous names, a handful of stars and teams stand out.

Perhaps the most famous name in sports from the 1920s is baseball player Babe Ruth, often referred to as the Sultan of Swat and the Bambino. George Herman Ruth (1895–1948) played for the Boston Red Sox (1914–19) and New York Yankees (1920–34). In 1920, he not only hit more home runs than any baseball player in history, he hit more home runs than any team in the American League that year. Then in 1927, he set a record that survived for more than three decades: 60 home runs, still the standard for sluggers.

Many fans believe that Ruth single-handedly saved baseball from the infamous Black Sox scandal of 1919. That year, eight members of the Chicago White Sox were accused of losing the World Series on purpose after being paid by gamblers. Although a jury acquitted them, the game's reputation was tarnished, but Ruth (with teammate Lou Gehrig) turned baseball into the most popular sport of the decade. The Bambino was a popular figure off the field as well. With his round, almost childlike face, his trademark camel-hair coat, and his easygoing manner, he was idolized by sports fans. Even his heavy drinking and high living seemed part of a likable zest for life.

Ruth was a heavy hitter, but so were some of the big-time boxers of the decade. One was William Harrison "Jack" Dempsey (1895–1983), who retired with 60 wins, 50 by knockout, 25 of those in the first round. He was born in Manassa, Colorado, and seemed destined for work in the local mines. But he showed a talent for boxing and eventually earned the nickname the Manassa Mauler. He burst on the national scene in 1919 when he won the heavyweight title. Throughout most of the 1920s, he was the top box-office draw in the sport. In 1921, he defeated French war hero Georges Carpentier, then defended his crown against Argentina's Luis Angel Firpo, known as the Bull of the Pampas. Firpo knocked Dempsey out of the ring in the first round, but sportswriters sitting ringside pushed him back in, and in the second round he won the fight with a knockout.

Dempsey's most celebrated fights, though, were the two he lost to another boxing legend, Gene Tunney, the Fighting Marine. In the first, on September 23, 1926, Dempsey lost his crown to Tunney. Their rematch came exactly one year later, before more than 104,000 fans in Chicago's Soldier Field. It remains one of the most famous bouts in boxing history because of its so-called long count. In round seven, Dempsey knocked Tunney to the mat. But instead of retreating to a neutral corner of the ring, Dempsey stood still until the referee's count of five (a boxer has until the count of 10 to get up and continue fighting). After ordering Dempsey to the corner, the referee then restarted the count. The extra time allowed Tunney to get to his feet on the count of 9—which was really "14"-and go on to win the fight. Dempsey's legion of fans believed he had been cheated.

If baseball was seen as a middle-class sport and boxing as a working-class sport, golf was the sport of the upper crust. They found a sports hero in Bobby Jones. Robert Tyre Jones Jr. (1902–71) was born in Atlanta, Georgia. He took up golf at age five, and by his late teens he had won a number of amateur tournaments. His temper kept him from winning a major golf tournament until 1923, when he controlled his emotions and won the U.S. Open. From then until 1930, he dominated the game as no golfer has since. He won the U.S. Open four times, the U.S. Amateur five times, the

Amateur golfer Bobby Jones dominated the sport throughout the 1920s.
(Private Collection)

GENTLEMAN JONES
Jones was renowned for his gentlemanly behavior. At the 1925 U.S. Open, his ball moved when he approached it near the 11th green. Over the objections of tournament officials, he insisted on taking a penalty stroke. Later, when someone complimented him on his sportsmanship, he replied, "You might as well praise me for not breaking into banks."

Bobby Jones nicknamed his putter Calamity Jane.

Possibly the most famous and widely reprinted sports photo of all time is this one of the legendary Four Horsemen, the football backfield at Notre Dame University.
(Notre Dame University)

Today, college and pro football players routinely top 200, even 300 pounds. The heaviest of the Four Horseman of Notre Dame weighed in at just 162 pounds.

British Open three times, and the British Amateur once. In 1930, he won all four of these titles, the first golfer ever to win golf's Grand Slam (the four major tournaments). In all, he won an astounding 62 percent of the major tournaments in which he played.

And he did it all for fun. Unlike most world-class athletes, he never turned professional. Further, he was one of the most highly educated sports stars in history, with degrees in mechanical engineering (Georgia Tech), literature (Harvard), and law (Emory University). After his playing days ended, he went on to a successful law career.

One of the most overpowering college football teams of any era was the Fighting Irish of Notre Dame in South Bend, Indiana. Under coaching legend Knute Rockne, the team compiled a record of 105 wins against just 12 losses and 5 ties in 13 years (1918–31). The team went undefeated in five of those seasons.

Among all that success, one Notre Dame game stands out. On October 18, 1924, the underdog Irish beat Army, then also a football powerhouse, 13 to 7. What is remembered more than the game itself is the *New York Herald-Tribune* story the next day. The story was written by Grantland Rice, the 1920s' most widely read sportswriter. In one of the most enduring passages in sports journalism, Rice began his account of the game:

Outlined against a blue-gray October sky the Four Horsemen rode again.

In dramatic lore they are known as Famine, Pestilence, Destruction and Death. These are only aliases. Their real names are: Stuhldreher, Miller, Crowley and Layden. They formed the crest of the South Bend cyclone before which another fighting Army team was swept over the precipice at the Polo Grounds this afternoon as 55,000 spectators peered down upon the bewildering panorama spread out upon the green plain below.

The Four Horsemen—figures described in the biblical Book of Revelation—were the four members of the Notre Dame backfield, who led the team to a 10-0 record and a national championship. The university's publicity department was determined to make the name stick. It took a photo of the four players posed on horses from a livery stable in town. The newspaper wire services picked up the photo and printed it in newspapers across the country. The legend of the Four Horsemen of Notre Dame, perhaps the greatest backfield in college football history, was born. Today it remains part of the mystique of Notre Dame football.

It would be many years before the color barrier would be broken in such sports as baseball and football. But that color barrier was at least partially cracked in the 1920s by the Harlem Renaissance basketball team, generally known as the Rens. The Rens were created by Bob Douglas, often called the Father of Black Basketball. Douglas struck a deal with New York City's Harlem Renaissance Casino in 1923. In exchange for use of a gym, Douglas gave the casino valuable free publicity by agreeing to call his team the Renaissance.

The Rens compiled a record that was nothing short of astounding. Over 26 years, the team racked up 2,588 wins and 529 losses. One season, the team went

Legendary coach Knute Rockne coached the Notre Dame football team to five undefeated seasons in the 1920s. *(Notre Dame University)*

ROCKNE'S ROCKETTES?

One reason for the Four Horsemen's success was its use of the backfield shift, a Rockne innovation. Rockne got the idea for the shift after watching chorus girls in a Chicago show. Impressed by their flawless timing and elegance, he concluded that he could put those characteristics to work in football.

BASEBALL SCANDAL

The Black Sox scandal has been the subject of popular films, including *Field of Dreams* (1989), based on W. P. Kinsella's novel *Shoeless Joe.* The movie stars Kevin Costner as an Iowa farmer who builds a baseball field in his cornfield. There, the ghost of "Shoeless Joe" Jackson, one of the game's greatest players, can redeem himself. For his role in the scandal, Jackson and his teammates were banned from baseball for life by baseball's commissioner Judge Kenesaw Mountain Landis.

Shoeless Joe Jackson, one of baseball's greatest players ever, was banned from the game for his role in the Black Sox betting scandal of 1919. *(Library of Congress)*

112 and 8. With such players as Frank Forbes, Fat Jenkins, Leon Mode, and Chuck "Tarzan" Cooper, the Rens competed with teams from the college, amateur, and all-white professional ranks. They were known for their extraordinary teamwork, dazzling passing ability, and showmanship. The team frequently went on barnstorming tours, playing day after day in smaller cities and towns throughout the East and Midwest. In some isolated towns, they were the first African Americans people had ever seen. Many youngsters were intrigued not only by their basketball talent but by their gear, for many had never seen a pair of athletic shoes. The Rens paved the way for the formation of the Harlem Globetrotters in 1927.

Although the Rens cracked the racial barrier, they did not break it. Many all-white teams respected their skills and gladly played against them. But team members still were not allowed to, for example, eat in local restaurants that refused to serve African Americans. The American Basketball League refused to admit them as members. In a show of support, the Original Celtics, the legendary all-white team from the 1920s and 1930s, refused to join the league, and the Rens and the Original Celtics formed an on-court rivalry that continued throughout the 1930s.

From the perspective of the 21st century, 1927 seems to be a watershed year. That year, Duke Ellington made his mark in Harlem, the first talkie was shown, Babe Ruth hit 60 home runs, Jack Dempsey lost his rematch with Gene Tunney, Bobby Jones published an autobiography entitled *Down the Fairway,* and the Harlem Globetrotters basketball team was formed. Led by the boom in car production, the economy was roaring.

CHAPTER 7

THE START OF THE HOOVER PRESIDENCY, 1928–1929

IN THE SUMMER OF 1927, CALVIN Coolidge was fishing in the Black Hills of South Dakota. On August 2, he called a press conference at a high school in nearby Rapid City. As the reporters filed into a classroom, the president handed each a slip of paper. Written on the paper were the words "I do not choose to run for President in nineteen twenty-eight." Silent Cal offered no further comment. At first, some reporters thought he was joking. But when they concluded that he was serious, they scrambled to the telephones to report the story to their editors. The field was open for a new face in the White House.

Calvin Coolidge (left) takes a last look at the White House as he rides to the inauguration of incoming president Herbert Hoover (right) in 1929. *(Library of Congress)*

Hoover's humanitarian efforts continued later in life. During the early years of the depression, he and the first lady often helped members of the White House staff by giving them money to pay their bills. After World War II, he raised $325 million to help starving and orphaned children in Europe.

Both Herbert and Lou Hoover spoke Chinese. At the White House they often spoke Chinese to each other to keep their conversations secret.

BACKGROUND ON HOOVER, THE HUMANITARIAN

The eventual winner of the 1928 presidential election was Herbert Hoover (1874–1964). While Hoover may have been a new face in the White House, he was already well known both in Washington politics and to the American public.

Hoover was born to Quaker parents in West Branch, Iowa, then a frontier settlement of just 325 people. His early life was difficult, among the most difficult of all U.S. presidents. In 1880, his father, a blacksmith, died at age 34. His mother took in sewing and taught school and Bible classes to support Herbert and his brother and sister for two years until she, too, died at age 34. The orphaned Hoover, just nine years of age, was put on a train to Oregon with 20 cents in his pocket. There he was raised by his stern Quaker uncle and aunt.

Hoover never graduated from high school. At age 14, he left school to work as an office boy in his uncle's land-sale company. He learned to type and do bookkeeping at a local night school. As a teenager he took a trip to the Cascade Mountains in the Northwest and was so enthused at seeing a mine that he decided he wanted to become a mining engineer. Although he failed most of his entrance examinations to Stanford University in California, a Quaker professor got him admitted. A private tutor brought him up to speed, and he earned his degree in engineering. Even as a student he showed the tycoon spirit that eventually made him a millionaire. He ran a laundry service, a baggage service, and a newspaper route, and he worked as a typist, a handyman, and a waiter. During his junior year, as class treasurer, he cleared the Stanford student association of its long-standing debts.

Hoover began his career in mining at age 21 working a 10-hour night shift at a Nevada gold mine for $1.50 a day. By age 23 he was managing a goldfield in Australia. His smart land purchases made fortunes for his British bosses and set him on the road to financial success. At age 24 he married Lou Henry, a geology student he had met at Stanford.

In the years that followed, the young married couple lived a life of pure adventure spiced with personal danger. The two traveled to China, where they were stranded during a rebellion. While Herbert was building barricades and walking guard duty, Lou was working as a nurse with a Mauser handgun stuck in her belt. At one point during the crisis, Hoover came to the aid of 600 trapped Chinese Christian refugees, getting food and water to them. Later, he found an ancient Chinese map that led him to an abandoned silver mine in the Asian country of Burma (now Myanmar). Ignoring the fresh tiger tracks in the mine, he reopened it and began to add to his fortune.

By 1918, Hoover had amassed a fortune of $4 million in the mining business. But as a Quaker, he was committed to humanitarian and charitable causes, so he turned his attention from increasing his wealth to public service. As a well-known business leader, he was appointed head of the Commission for Relief in Belgium after World War I erupted in Europe. Through his efforts, 7 million hungry Belgians impoverished by the fighting and destruction received food. Hoover paid for much of this food out of his own personal fortune. At the risk of death from German submarine warfare, he repeatedly crossed the Atlantic to administer the relief effort. Even the hostile German government acknowledged the importance of his work: German authorities wrote on his passport, "This man is not to be stopped anywhere under any circumstances." After

Herbert Hoover and his wife, Lou Henry, lived an adventurous life before they took up residence in the White House. *(Library of Congress)*

FIRST FOR THE FIRST LADY

Lou Hoover recorded a number of firsts. She was the first woman to major in geology at Stanford University. She was the first national president of the Girl Scouts. She gave the first radio address by a first lady, speaking to children about how to cope with the Great Depression, and she was the first first lady to inventory the contents of the White House.

Before he was elected president, Herbert Hoover (left) was already well known to the American public as secretary of commerce in the Harding and Coolidge cabinets. *(Library of Congress)*

the war, Hoover served as director general of the postwar American Relief Administration. He led the effort to get food to Russians starving in the wake of the war and the Russian Revolution. It is no exaggeration to say that Hoover may have saved more people from a slow death by starvation than anyone in history.

These activities made Hoover a popular figure. In 1920, both the Republican and Democratic parties tried to enlist him as a candidate for president, but he refused to run. Instead, as secretary of commerce in the Harding and Coolidge cabinets, he was among the most capable and successful of these presidents' appointments. Almost single-handedly, he turned the U.S. Department of Commerce into a key federal agency. As secretary, he promoted the radio and airline industries, which were in their infancy. Bringing his engineer's mind to public policy, he pushed for standard measurements for industrial products; for example, because of Hoover, any standard lightbulb would fit into any standard socket. He established safety rules for railroads, automobiles, elevators, and other products, and he led the effort to develop stricter building codes to make homes and buildings safer.

By 1927, Hoover had earned a national reputation as a public administrator, a philanthropist, and a business leader. He represented the American ideal of the self-made millionaire. So when Coolidge chose not to run for a second full term, Hoover threw his hat into the ring and easily won the Republican Party nomination.

Within a week of Smith's nomination, 10 million anti-Catholic handbills, leaflets, posters, and pamphlets had been distributed. The source of most of these was the KKK.

CAMPAIGN OPPONENT AL SMITH AND THE RISE OF THE DEMOCRATS

Although Hoover won the 1928 presidential election by a large majority, the campaign was a spirited one and voter turnout was high. One reason for the high turnout was that the Democratic Party nominated a colorful and outspoken candidate, New York governor Al Smith.

Alfred Emanuel Smith (1873–1944) had been a leading candidate for the Democratic nomination in 1924. His name had been placed in nomination by future president Franklin D. Roosevelt, who called Smith "the happy warrior, the man whom strong men in arms would wish to be." The party that year, though, was sharply divided, so Smith was never able to emerge as the nominee and the party settled for compromise candidate John Davis. Four years later, the party could no longer deny Smith the nomination.

Historians regard the Happy Warrior as one of the most intriguing politicians in U.S. history. He was born and raised on the Lower East Side of New York City, where as a child he watched the construction of the Brooklyn Bridge. Smith represented the American melting pot: his mother was Irish, his father was Italian and German. He dropped out of school at age 12 to earn money selling groceries, delivering newspapers, and working long hours at the Fulton Street fish market. He hung out with tough street kids, but he was also an altar boy at the St. James Catholic Church.

By his early twenties, Smith was hanging around with a different crowd, members of the New York City political organization known as Tammany Hall. Tammany Hall was a loose association of people with political influence. Formed in 1789, it was originally a charity for the city's poor and immigrant population. Over time, though, it became more and more involved with local politics, and during certain periods, it practically ran New York City. It sometimes relied on corruption and bribes, but it always relied on granting

Democrat Al Smith, the first Catholic presidential candidate, ran a spirited campaign for the White House in 1928. *(Library of Congress)*

At the time Smith was appointed to the legislature's committee on banking, he had never entered a bank—because he never had enough money to open account.

In the days before air travel was common, presidential candidates like Al Smith (in bowler hat) had to travel from city to city by train. *(Library of Congress)*

During the campaign, Hoover was never heard to mention Smith's name, even once, in public.

Al Smith was an appealing presidential candidate, but he was unable to overcome Herbert Hoover's immense popularity as a businessman and humanitarian. *(Library of Congress)*

favors—and expected those favors to be returned. To this day, the name Tammany Hall is synonymous with big-city political bosses who get and hold power by doling out favors to friends and supporters.

With the help of the Tammany bosses, Smith got his first job in politics, working for the commissioner of jurors. He then was elected to the state legislature, where he served from 1903 to 1915. Then in 1918 he began a two-year term as governor of New York. His lost his reelection bid in 1920, but in 1922 he won the first of three more consecutive terms as governor. While he was a product of the Tammany machine, he rose above it and governed New York with an honest hand. He gave top jobs not to cronies but to those who were best qualified. He believed that the state, not the church or political bosses, was responsible for social welfare and reform, so he instituted such policies as pensions for widows and a 48-hour workweek for women and children—at a time when men, women, and children routinely worked much longer hours. He had little patience for the Red scares of the early 1920s.

Hoover and Smith could not have been more unlike. Smith was a product of the big city. Hoover was from a small town in the Midwest. Smith, the school dropout, was outgoing, with a casual manner, sometimes creative grammar, and a thick New York accent. He was a snappy dresser, and he liked to make wisecracks between puffs on a big cigar. Hoover, the well-spoken college graduate, was somewhat stiff in manner and dressed in a way that reflected his conservative Quaker roots; even while fishing, he wore a necktie. Smith was a feisty campaigner, at home in front of a crowd and easygoing with people of any nationality and race, though he tended to freeze up in front of a radio microphone. Hoover, who had a rich, appealing radio voice, ran a quiet campaign, refusing to attack his opponent, and he knew little of African Americans or immigrants. Smith was a wet, opposed to Prohibition. Hoover was a dry, although he did enjoy a drink occasionally in private (and, despite his religious upbringing, was known to be able to swear with the best of his miners). Most important, Smith was Catholic—the first Catholic nominee by a major party in presidential election history. Hoover, a Quaker, was a champion of small-town religious fundamentalism.

These personal differences strongly reflected the divisions that had run through the country in 1924 and continued to divide voters. The economy was growing

The Empire State Building, on which construction began in 1929, is one of the most recognizable landmarks on the New York City skyline. *(Library of Congress)*

THE SKYSCRAPER

Al Smith lost the election. He went on to help establish a landmark as president of the company that built the Empire State Building in New York City.

The most distinctive American architectural form of the 1920s was the skyscraper. These tall buildings represented the nation's infatuation with things that were newer, bigger, and better. Skyscrapers were changing the skylines of many American cities, including Cleveland, Pittsburgh, San Francisco, Kansas City, and others. By 1929, there were 377 skyscrapers of more than 20 stories in height throughout the nation.

One of the most famous skyscrapers was—and is—the Empire State Building. Construction began in 1929, and when it was completed, it was the winner in the race to be the tallest building in the world. In 1929, the Bank of Manhattan was the tallest building; in 1930, the Chrysler Building in New York City took that title. The Empire State Building, constructed at a feverish pace in just two years, became the tallest building in the world in 1931 at 1,250 feet (1,453 feet 8⁹⁄₁₆ inches to the top of the building's lightning rod). At its peak, 3,000 men worked on the construction of the building.

On Wednesday, October 30, 1929, newspapers reported the October 29 stock market crash that signaled the start of the Great Depression. *(Library of Congress)*

WINDOW ON WALL STREET
It is popularly believed that a wave of suicides accompanied the stock market crash as desperate investors jumped out of windows of office buildings in New York City. That suicide increase did not happen. Statistics show that the number of suicides nationally in October and November was actually lower than the number during the summer, when stock prices were still rising.

and the nation was at peace, so in the minds of many voters, the election was a choice between big city/wet/Irish Catholic and rural/dry/fundamentalist.

The Smith candidacy was doomed from the start. Throughout much of the country, he was almost a foreigner. He was deeply troubled by the distrust of his religion. Like Catholic president John F. Kennedy some three decades later, he had to repeatedly assure voters that his allegiance was to the Constitution of the United States, not to Rome and the pope. In many places, anti-Catholic prejudice ran deep: On the night of September 19, 1928, as his campaign train crossed into Oklahoma, he was greeted by Ku Klux Klan crosses burning on either side of the tracks.

Further, the economic boom under the Republicans allowed Hoover to campaign under the slogan "A chicken in every pot and a car in every garage." Smith might have been able to take more advantage of the ongoing depression in the farm industry, but the accent of the Irish Catholic candidate from New York City grated on the ears of Protestant farmers in rural states such as Kansas and Oklahoma. When the votes were counted, Hoover (with running mate Charles Curtis of Kansas) had won with 21.4 million votes to Smith's 15 million.

SHARED MISFORTUNE

The 1920s began with deep divisions between the American people. Some were socialists; others were capitalists. There were wets and drys, rural conservatives and urban sophisticates, blacks and whites. Ironically, the Great Depression actually brought some of these people together in shared misfortune. In his 1970 book *Hard Times,* author Studs Terkel records the experiences of the thousands of tramps and drifters who traveled the country during the depression. Here are the words of one such drifter:

Black and white, it didn't make any difference who you were, 'cause everybody was poor. All friendly, sleep in a jungle [hobo camp]. We used to take a big pot and cook food, cabbage, meat and beans all together. We all set together, we made a tent. Twenty-five or thirty would be out on the side of the rail, white and colored. They didn't have no mothers or sisters, they didn't have no home, they were dirty, they had overalls on, they didn't have no food, they didn't have anything.

Although Hoover's victory was resounding, Smith's campaign reenergized the Democratic Party. He won far more votes than any other Democratic candidate had in the 20th century, including President Wilson. He also carried the nation's 12 largest cities, in contrast to 1924, when the Republicans won in all 12 of those cities. Four years later, after the economic boom had ended, more rural voters joined workers in those cities to elect a Democrat, Franklin D. Roosevelt, to the first of his four terms in the White House.

Herbert Hoover was the first U.S. president born west of the Mississippi River.

STOCK MARKET CRASH OF 1929 AND THE START OF THE GREAT DEPRESSION

During his campaign, Hoover said, "Given a chance to go forward with the policies of the last eight years…poverty will be banished from the nation." Hoover could not have been more wrong.

Hoover's name, perhaps unfairly, is forever linked with the onset of the Great Depression. This is the name given to the severe economic downturn that persisted from 1929 until U.S. entry into World War II in 1941 but was at its worst from 1929 to 1933. During Hoover's single term in office during these years, 90,000 businesses failed. The gross national product—the value of all goods and services produced in the country—fell by a

BIG LOSERS

Many prominent people lost big on the stock market. Singer Fanny Brice lost $500,000. Attorney Clarence Darrow, who increased his fame in the Scopes Monkey Trial, was left almost penniless. Comedians Groucho Marx and his brother Harpo each lost about a quarter million dollars. The big losers were the Vanderbilt family, which lost $40 million on its railroad stocks, and financier J. Pierpont Morgan, who lost up to $60 million.

The words *teenage* and *teenager* were rarely used before about 1920. Until then, people in their teens were referred to as youngsters or individually as a young man or a young woman.

The sadness of this depression-era boy, photographed in Westmoreland County, Pennsylvania, in 1936, gives some indication of the hardships Americans endured during the 1930s. *(Library of Congress)*

third. The family incomes of farmers fell by half, those of factory workers by over a third. The number of unemployed rose from under a million to about 15 million—25 percent of the workforce. The production of steel fell to just 12 percent of the industry's capacity. It was the most devastating, widespread collapse of the economy in American history.

The most startling event of the Great Depression was the stock market crash in October 1929, just months after Hoover's inauguration. Throughout the 1920s the stock market had been steadily rising, but in 1928 a kind of mania had taken over. Between March and November that year, the price of one share of stock in the Radio Corporation of America (RCA) rose from under $100 to $400. By September 1929, the stock topped $500. Stock in General Electric, $128 in March 1928, rose to nearly $400 over the same period. U.S. Steel rose from $138 to $279.

More and more people were pouring their savings into the stock market, thinking that they, too, could get rich. Many of them were buying stock on margin. An investor who buys on margin has to put up only a fraction of the stock's price and borrows the rest from the brokerage house selling the stock. Thus, a person buying a $100 stock could put up just $10; if the stock went to $110, the investor could sell and make $10 on a $10 investment, a return of 100 percent. But stocks were doubling and tripling in value. Those fortunate enough to sell in time earned dizzyingly high returns. In the summer of 1929, *The Wall Street Journal,* the most important financial newspaper in the country, wrote, "The outlook for the fall months seems brighter than at any time."

The stock market reached its highest point on September 3, 1929. The bubble was bound to burst. On September 5, prices went down sharply, but the market recovered the next day. On into October, stock prices wavered. Then on Black Thursday, October 24, a wave of panic selling—of about 13 million shares—sent

After the affluence of the Roaring Twenties, many unemployed people had to stand in bread lines such as this one just to get food. *(Brown Brothers)*

prices down. On Friday, some of the nation's wealthiest financiers tried to stop the panic selling by placing large buy orders. On Monday, though, prices fell again, and the stock market overall lost $14 billion.

Tuesday, October 29, was the worst day in stock market history to that time. That day 16 million shares were sold, and the stock prices of such companies as General Electric, International Harvester, American Telephone & Telegraph, and U.S. Steel collapsed. Part of the problem was that investors who had bought on margin were receiving margin calls from their brokers. A dreaded margin call requires the investor to put up more money for the stock to keep the overall value of the account at the same level as it was before the price went down. The only way many investors had to raise the money was to sell stock. But by selling stock, they sent prices even lower in a downward spiral.

A stock market crash and an economic depression, though, are not the same thing. Only about 1.5 million Americans owned stock, and only about 600,000 of those were active stock traders. The stock market crash did not cause the depression. Rather, the crash was a symptom of a number of weaknesses in the economy.

"Tragedy, despair, and ruination spell the story of countless thousands of marginal stock traders. Perhaps Manhattan was worst hit in the number of victims."

—Front-page, *Variety,* Wednesday, October 30, 1929

The number of bank failures rose steadily throughout the Hoover administration. In 1929, 659 banks failed. The number rose to 1,352 in 1930, 1,456 in 1931, 2,294 in 1932, and 5,190 in 1933. In many parts of the country, the police had to turn away angry mobs that were trying to get their money out of the banks.

However, it was important as much for its psychological impact as its economic impact. For in October 1929, the Roaring Twenties came to an end. Almost overnight Americans lost faith that financially, life would just get better and better.

At its root, the Great Depression was caused by overproduction—that is, American businesses were producing more than Americans could buy. The 1920s marked the first decade of modern mass production and mass consumerism. But with wages and farm profits remaining low, too many people could not afford to buy the cars, refrigerators, radios, and other products that were rolling off the assembly lines. Many of those who did buy these products bought them on credit. When employers had to start laying off workers, many of these workers could no longer afford to pay their debts. Making matters worse, the banks that had loaned them money lost millions of dollars in bad debts, so they, too, failed, taking with them the savings of other customers. Now these people had no money to buy products or pay their debts, making the situation worsen in yet another downward spiral. With fewer and fewer buyers for their goods, factories laid off more workers, setting the spiral in motion again.

Another major cause of the depression was that wealth was not evenly distributed. The 1920s were roaring for some people but a struggle for many farmers and industrial workers. During the 1920s productivity in factories went up 43 percent, but wages rose hardly at all. Farm prices fell throughout the decade. Billions and billions of dollars went not to increasing wages but to stock market speculation. The result was too much wealth in the hands of too few people. If some of that money had gone to higher wages, workers would have been able to buy more goods. Production and buying would then have been more in balance. As things were, the excess and greed of the Roaring Twenties led to economic collapse.

African Americans, American Indians, and Hispanics were among the hardest hit. Many African Americans had moved north to find jobs in factories, but as recent hires, they were the first to be laid off. Many Mexican immigrants met the same fate. American Indians who had moved to cities to work during a building boom lost their jobs as construction ceased suddenly. But everyone was affected. Middle-class and affluent college students had to drop out because their families had lost everything. People stopped seeking medical care because they had no money, so doctors and dentists fell on hard times. War veterans were selling pencils and apples on street corners. Millions of people subsisted on a diet of thin soup and beans while produce rotted in the fields because prices were too low to make harvesting worthwhile. They combed through slag heaps looking for chips of coal to heat their homes, while nearby stood idle machinery that had enabled them to mine more coal in five minutes than they could find in a day.

The 1920s began with a promise of a return to "normalcy." It progressed with a promise that science, technology, and industry would bring a better life to millions. By the end of the decade, Americans were singing along with the popular tune "Ain't We Got Fun." The fun ended, and starting in late 1929 Americans hunkered down to face 16 years of depression and another world war.

"Terrible sights. Terrible sounds. Sitting there hour after hour, watching my own "investments" shrink and shrivel, my heart ached for the poor people around me."

—From a description of the Wall Street panic in "Now I've Gone Back to Work" in *American Magazine*, February 1930

GLOSSARY

anarchist   A person who does not believe in government. Often used to refer to those who advocated the violent overthrow of the U.S. government in the 1920s.

Bolshevik   Communist political party that seized power in Russia after the 1917 Russian Revolution; sometimes used as a synonym for communist.

capitalism   An economic system that calls for private ownership of the means of production, as well as the profits from production.

Charleston   A popular dance craze in the 1920s.

communism   An economic system opposed to capitalism by advocating the abolition of private property and private business profits.

Eighteenth Amendment   The 1919 amendment to the U.S. Constitution that banned the "manufacture, sale, or transportation of intoxicating liquors."

flapper   Term used in the 1920s to refer a new type of woman who defied the conventions of behavior of earlier generations.

Great Depression   The sharp downturn in the U.S. economy from 1929 to 1941.

Great Migration   The widespread movement of African Americans to the North and Midwest in the 1910s and 1920s.

gross national product   The total value of goods and services produced in the country, used as a measure of the economy's productivity.

Harlem Renaissance   The reawakening of pride and consciousness in the African American community, often reflected in the work of artists and writers who gravitated to Harlem, New York.

jazz   A form of popular music, originating in the African-American community, that emphasizes syncopated rhythms, a pulsing beat, and improvisation (creating music on the spot without a fixed score).

Ku Klux Klan   An organization formed in 1866 to resist Reconstruction in the South after the Civil War and revived in the 1910s. Known particularly for its racial intimidation and opposition to African Americans, Catholics, and Jews.

laissez-faire   A French expression commonly used to describe an economic system, or any system, that is allowed to run itself without interference, particularly from government.

Meriam Report   A 1928 report for the federal government on American Indian affairs. The report pronounced the policies of the preceding 50 years a failure, documented the poor conditions of the reservations and boarding schools, and pointed out the schools' destructive effects on American Indian culture and students' self-esteem.

National Origins Act   Law restricting immigration passed in 1924.

National Prohibition Enforcement Act (Volstead Act)   The 1919 law, commonly called the Volstead Act, passed to enforce the Eighteenth Amendment outlawing the manufacture and sale of liquor.

Nineteenth Amendment   The 1920 amendment to the U.S. Constitution granting women the right to vote.

prohibition   General term for the federal laws and constitutional amendment making the manufacture and sale of liquor illegal from 1919 to 1933.

ratification   The process by which the states approve an amendment to the U.S. Constitution or the U.S. Senate approves an international treaty.

Red scares   Term applied to a general fear of communism, socialism, and anarchy in the late 1910s and early 1920s.

Sherman Antitrust Act   A 1890 law that made illegal any "contract, combination, . . . or conspiracy, in restraint of trade or commerce among the several States." The act was intended to curb monopoly businesses, but it was often used as a tool against labor unions in the 1910s and 1920s.

socialism   An economic and social philosophy that calls for state ownership of industry and a more equal distribution of wealth, usually within a capitalist system that allows private profits.

speakeasy   Hidden clubs where liquor was illegally sold during Prohibition.

tariff   A duty, or tax, levied on imported goods. Tariffs make goods imported from other countries more expensive, so they help increase the demand for goods made at home.

Universal Negro Improvement Association   Organization formed by Marcus Garvey; the largest black nonreligious organization in African-American history.

FURTHER READING

BOOKS

Allen, Frederick Lewis. *Only Yesterday: An Informal History of the 1920s*. New York: Wiley, 1997.

American Heritage History of the '20s and '30s. New York: American Heritage, 1970.

Avrich, Paul. *Sacco and Vanzetti*. Princeton, N.J.: Princeton University Press, 1996.

Botshon, Lisa, and Meredith Goldsmith. *Middlebrow Moderns: Popular American Women Writers of the 1920s*. Boston: Northeastern University Press, 2003.

Commager, Henry Steele, ed. *The American Destiny*. Vol. 13, *The Twenties*. London: Orbis, 1986.

Divine, Robert A., T. H. Breen, George M. Fredrickson, and R. Hall Williams. *America: Past and Present,* 2d ed. Glenview, Ill.: Scott, Foresman, 1987.

Dumenil, Lynn, and Eric Foner. *The Modern Temper: American Culture and Society in the 1920s*. New York: Hill and Wang, 1995.

Evans, Harold. *The American Century*. New York: Knopf, 1998.

Fass, Paula. *The Damned and the Beautiful: American Youth in the 1920s*. New York: Oxford University Press, 1979.

Feinstein, Stephen. *The 1920s: From Prohibition to Charles Lindbergh*. Berkeley, N.J.: Enslow, 2001.

Ferrell, Robert H. *The Presidency of Calvin Coolidge*. Lawrence: University Press of Kansas, 1998.

Foner, Eric, and John A. Garraty, eds. *The Reader's Companion to American History*. Boston: Houghton Mifflin, 1991.

Frankfurter, Marion D., ed. *The Letters of Sacco and Vanzetti*. New York: Penguin, 1997.

Goldberg, David J. *Discontented America: The United States in the 1920s*. Baltimore, Md.: Johns Hopkins University Press, 1999.

Grossman, James R. *Land of Hope: Chicago, Black Southerners, and the Great Migration*. Chicago: University of Chicago Press, 1989.

Hakim, Joy. *War, Peace, and All That Jazz*. New York: Oxford University Press, 1995.

Hanson, Erica. *A Cultural History of the United States through the Decades: The 1920s*. San Diego, Calif.: Lucent, 1999.

Herald, Jacqueline. *Fashions of a Decade: The 1920s*. New York: Facts On File, 1991.

Kobler, John. *Ardent Spirits: The Rise and Fall of Prohibition*. New York: Putnam, 1973.

Leuchtenburg, William E. *The Perils of Prosperity, 1914–1932*. Chicago: University of Chicago Press, 1993.

Lewis, David L. *When Harlem Was in Vogue*. New York: Knopf, 1981.

Lieurance, Suzanne. *Prohibition Era in American History*. Berkeley Heights: N.J.: Enslow, 2003.

May, Ernest R. *The* Life *History of the United States*. Vol. 10: 1917–1932. *Boom and Bust*. New York: Time-Life Books, 1964.

Miller, Nathan. *New World Coming: The 1920s and the Making of Modern America*. New York: Scribner, 2003.

Murray, Robert K. *The Politics of Normalcy: Governmental Theory and Practice in the Harding-Coolidge Era*. New York: Norton, 1973.

Noggle, Burl. *Teapot Dome: Oil and Politics in the 1920s*. Westport, Conn.: Greenwood Press, 1980.

Pietrusza, David. *Roaring Twenties*. Detroit: Gale Group, 1998.

Russel, Francis. *The Shadow of Blooming Grove: Warren G. Harding in His Times*. New York: McGraw-Hill, 1968.

Schneider, Mark Robert. *We Return Fighting: The Civil Rights Movement in the Jazz Age*. Evanston, Ill.: Northeastern University Press, 2001.

Schowalter, Elaine. *These Modern Women: Autobiographical Essays from the Twenties*. New York: Feminist Press, 1989.

Smith, Page. *Redeeming the Time: A People's History of the 1920s and the New Deal*. New York: McGraw-Hill, 1986.

Smulyan, Susan. *Selling Radio: The Commercialization of American Broadcasting, 1920–1934*. Washington, D.C.: Smithsonian Books, 1996.

Sobel, Robert. *Coolidge*. Washington, D.C.: Regnery, 2000.

Stolley, Richard B., ed. *Our Century in Pictures*. Boston: Little Brown, n.d.

Time-Life editors. *End of Innocence, 1910–1920*. New York: Time-Life Books, 2000.

Williams, Martin. *The Jazz Tradition*. New York: Oxford University Press, 1993.

Wilson, Joan Hoff. *Herbert Hoover: Forgotten Progressive*. Prospect Heights, Ill.: Waveland Press, 1992.

Yancey, Diane. *Life During the Roaring Twenties*. Detroit: Gale Group, 2002.

WEB SITES

Killeen Harker Heights Connections. "American History," Available online. URL: http://killeenroos.com/link/amhist.htm#Roaring. Updated on July 14, 2001.

Kingwood College Library. "American Cultural History 1920–1929," Available online. URL: http://kclibrary.nhmccd.edu/ decade20.html. Updated in May 2002.

PSCST. "The 1920s Experience," Available online. URL: http://www.angelfire.com/co/pscst. Downloaded on February 10, 2004.

Teacher Oz. "20th and 21st Century America: The Roaring Twenties," Available online. URL: http://www.teacheroz.com/20thcent.htm#20s. Updated in January 2004.

INDEX